Education in a Competitive and Globalizing World

K-12 Education Challenges

Employees with Sexual Misconduct Histories and Students Who Change Schools

EDUCATION IN A COMPETITIVE AND GLOBALIZING WORLD

Additional books in this series can be found on Nova's website under the Series tab.

Additional E-books in this series can be found on Nova's website under the E-books tab.

EDUCATION IN A COMPETITIVE AND GLOBALIZING WORLD

K-12 EDUCATION CHALLENGES

EMPLOYEES WITH SEXUAL MISCONDUCT HISTORIES AND STUDENTS WHO CHANGE SCHOOLS

ANDREW J. HERNANDEZ
AND
SETH L. JORDAN
EDITORS

Nova Science Publishers, Inc.
New York

Copyright © 2012 by Nova Science Publishers, Inc.

All rights reserved. No part of this book may be reproduced, stored in a retrieval system or transmitted in any form or by any means: electronic, electrostatic, magnetic, tape, mechanical photocopying, recording or otherwise without the written permission of the Publisher.

For permission to use material from this book please contact us:
Telephone 631-231-7269; Fax 631-231-8175
Web Site: http://www.novapublishers.com

NOTICE TO THE READER

The Publisher has taken reasonable care in the preparation of this book, but makes no expressed or implied warranty of any kind and assumes no responsibility for any errors or omissions. No liability is assumed for incidental or consequential damages in connection with or arising out of information contained in this book. The Publisher shall not be liable for any special, consequential, or exemplary damages resulting, in whole or in part, from the readers' use of, or reliance upon, this material. Any parts of this book based on government reports are so indicated and copyright is claimed for those parts to the extent applicable to compilations of such works.

Independent verification should be sought for any data, advice or recommendations contained in this book. In addition, no responsibility is assumed by the publisher for any injury and/or damage to persons or property arising from any methods, products, instructions, ideas or otherwise contained in this publication.

This publication is designed to provide accurate and authoritative information with regard to the subject matter covered herein. It is sold with the clear understanding that the Publisher is not engaged in rendering legal or any other professional services. If legal or any other expert assistance is required, the services of a competent person should be sought. FROM A DECLARATION OF PARTICIPANTS JOINTLY ADOPTED BY A COMMITTEE OF THE AMERICAN BAR ASSOCIATION AND A COMMITTEE OF PUBLISHERS.

Additional color graphics may be available in the e-book version of this book.

Library of Congress Cataloging-in-Publication Data

ISBN 978-1-61942-870-6

Published by Nova Science Publishers, Inc. † *New York*

CONTENTS

Preface   **vii**

Chapter 1   K-12 Education: Selected Cases of Public
and Private Schools That Hired or Retained
Individuals with Histories of Sexual Misconduct   **1**
United States Government Accountability Office

Chapter 2   K-12 Education: Many Challenges Arise in
Educating Students Who Change Schools Frequently   **53**
United States Government Accountability Office

Index   **101**

PREFACE

This book examines the circumstances surrounding cases where K-12 schools hired or retained individuals with histories of sexual misconduct and determines the factors contributing to such employment actions. An overview of selected federal and state laws related to the employment of convicted sex offenders in K-12 schools is reviewed. Additionally, many challenges arise in educating students who change schools frequently. Research suggests that mobility is one of several interrelated factors, such as socio-economic status and lack of parental education, which have a negative effect of academic achievement. The recent economic downturn, with foreclosures and homeless-ness, may be increasing student mobility.

Chapter 1 - Prior GAO testimonies have described cases of physical abuse of children at youth residential treatment programs and public and private schools. However, children are also vulnerable to sexual abuse. A 2004 Department of Education report estimated that millions of students are subjected to sexual misconduct by a school employee at some time between kindergarten and the twelfth grade (K-12).

GAO was asked to (1) examine the circumstances surrounding cases where K-12 schools hired or retained individuals with histories of sexual misconduct and determine the factors contributing to such employment actions and (2) provide an overview of selected federal and state laws related to the employment of convicted sex offenders in K-12 schools.

To identify case studies, GAO compared 2007 to 2009 data employment databases from 19 states and the District of Columbia to data in the National Sex Offender Registry. GAO also searched public records from 2000 to 2010 to identify cases in which sexual misconduct by school employees ultimately resulted in a criminal conviction. GAO ultimately selected 15 cases from 11 states for further investigation. For each case, to the extent possible, GAO reviewed court documents and personnel files and also interviewed relevant school officials and law enforcement. GAO reviewed applicable federal and state laws related to the employment of sex offenders and requirements for conducting criminal history checks.

Chapter 2 - Educational achievement of students can be negatively affected by their changing schools often. The recent economic downturn, with foreclosures and homelessness, may be increasing student mobility.

To inform Elementary and Secondary Education Act of 1965 (ESEA) reauthorization, GAO was asked: (1) What are the numbers and characteristics of students who change schools, and what are the reasons students change schools? (2)What is known about the effects of mobility on student outcomes, including academic achievement, behavior, and other outcomes? (3) What challenges does student mobility present for schools in meeting the educational needs of students who change schools? (4) What key federal programs are schools using to address the needs of mobile students? GAO analyzed federal survey data, interviewed U.S. Department of Education (Education) officials, conducted site visits at eight schools in six school districts, and reviewed federal laws and existing research.

In: K-12 Education Challenges
Editors: A.Hernandez and S. Jordan

ISBN 978-1-61942-870-6
© 2012 Nova Science Publishers, Inc.

Chapter 1

K-12 Education: Selected Cases of Public and Private Schools That Hired or Retained Individuals with Histories of Sexual Misconduct*

United States Government Accountability Office

Why GAO Did This Study

Prior GAO testimonies have described cases of physical abuse of children at youth residential treatment programs and public and private schools. However, children are also vulnerable to sexual abuse. A 2004 Department of Education report estimated that millions of students are subjected to sexual misconduct by a school employee at some time between kindergarten and the twelfth grade (K-12).

GAO was asked to (1) examine the circumstances surrounding cases where K-12 schools hired or retained individuals with histories of sexual misconduct and determine the factors contributing to such employment actions and (2) provide an overview of selected federal and state laws related to the employment of convicted sex offenders in K-12 schools.

To identify case studies, GAO compared 2007 to 2009 data employment databases from 19 states and the District of Columbia to data in the National Sex Offender Registry. GAO also searched public records from 2000 to 2010 to identify cases in which sexual misconduct by school employees ultimately resulted in a criminal conviction. GAO ultimately selected 15 cases from 11

2   United States Government Accountability Office

states for further investigation. For each case, to the extent possible, GAO reviewed court documents and personnel files and also interviewed relevant school officials and law enforcement. GAO reviewed applicable federal and state laws related to the employment of sex offenders and requirements for conducting criminal history checks.

WHAT GAO FOUND

The 15 cases GAO examined show that individuals with histories of sexual misconduct were hired or retained by public and private schools as teachers, support staff, volunteers, and contractors.

Examples of Cases GAO Examined

School and dates of employment	Case details
Multiple Ohio public schools, August 1993 to May 2006	• Although forced to resign because of inappropriate conduct with female students, this teacher received a letter of recommendation from the school superintendent calling him an "outstanding teacher." • He was subsequently hired at a neighboring district, where he was convicted for sexual battery against a sixth grade girl.
Multiple Louisiana schools, June 2006 to October 2007	• A teacher and registered sex offender whose Texas teaching certificate had been revoked was hired by several Louisiana schools without receiving a criminal history check. • A warrant is currently out for his arrest on charges of engaging in sexual conversations with a student at one of these schools.
Arizona public school, August 2001 to January 2002	• In a rush to fill a position, this school did not conduct a criminal history check before hiring a teacher who had been convicted for sexually abusing a minor, even though he disclosed on his application that he had committed a dangerous crime against a child. • He was later convicted for having sexual contact with a young female student; videos of nude underage girls were found in his possession.
California public school, August 1998 to October 2010	• In 2000, the offender was convicted for molesting a minor; the school was aware of his conviction but did not fire him. • After GAO referred the case to the California Attorney General, officials placed the offender on administrative leave. He has since resigned.

Source: Records including police reports, court documents, and interviews.

At least 11 of these 15 cases involve offenders who previously targeted children. Even more disturbing, in at least 6 cases, offenders used their new positions as school employees or volunteers to abuse more children. GAO found that the following factors contributed to hiring or retention: (1) school officials allowed teachers who had engaged in sexual misconduct toward students to resign rather than face disciplinary action, often providing subsequent employers with positive references; (2) schools did not perform preemployment criminal history checks; (3) even if schools did perform these checks, they may have been inadequate in that they were not national, fingerprint-based, or recurring; and (4) schools failed to inquire into troubling information regarding criminal histories on employment applications. The previous table contains information on 4 of GAO's 15 cases.

GAO found no federal laws regulating the employment of sex offenders in public or private schools and widely divergent laws at the state level. For example, some states require a national, fingerprint-based criminal history check for school employment, while others do not. State laws also vary as to whether past convictions must result in termination from school employment, revocation of a teaching license, or refusal to hire.

December 8, 2010
The Honorable George Miller
Chairman
Committee on Education and Labor
House of Representatives

Dear Mr. Chairman:

We have previously reported that children are being physically abused at youth residential treatment programs and at public and private schools.[1] Without question, vulnerable children are also victims of sexual abuse. Nationwide, more than 620,000 convicted sex offenders are either incarcerated, on probation, or residing freely in localities across the United States, according to an estimate by the National Center for Missing and Exploited Children.[2] This large and growing population of convicted offenders has raised public concerns in part because the victims of sexual assaults are more likely to be children; most offenders live in communities rather than in prison; and some sex offenders, particularly those who go without treatment, are at greater risk of committing another offense.[3] But convicted offenders and their victims represent just a fraction of the problem. In 2004, troubling surveys documented by the Department of Education estimated that millions of students are subjected to sexual misconduct by a school employee sometime between kindergarten and the twelfth grade (K-12). Interviews with actual offenders corroborate such statistics; one series of studies found that 232 child molesters admitted to molesting a total of 17,000 victims. In these cases, the individuals molested dozens, hundreds, and even thousands of victims, sometimes without ever being caught. In this context, you asked us to explore how these individuals obtain and maintain contact with school children. Specifically, you asked that we (1) examine the circumstances surrounding cases where K-12 schools hired or retained individuals with histories of sexual misconduct and determine the factors contributing to such employment actions and (2) provide an overview of selected federal and state laws related to the employment of sex offenders in K-12 public and private schools.

To select our case studies, we compared social security numbers (SSN) in the Department of Justice's (DOJ) National Sex Offender Registry (NSOR) to SSNs in employment databases maintained by 19 states and the District of Columbia[4] and covering approximately the years 2007 to 2009.[5] From this comparison, we identified hundreds of potential cases of registered sex offenders working in schools.[6] For each of these cases, we attempted to validate the identity of the offender and verify that their term of employment was after their conviction for a sex offense by using public records searches and contacting employers. We did not conduct any further investigation if we could not confirm that a registered sex offender had gained or retained employment at a school following their conviction. We also searched public records and identified dozens of cases from 2000 to 2010 in which sexual misconduct by school employees ultimately resulted in a criminal conviction. We then interviewed related parties, including current and former school officials, law enforcement officials, and representatives from state agencies to investigate the factors contributing to the hire or retention of the individuals in these cases. Where applicable, we reviewed police reports, witness statements, court documents, offenders' personnel files, and employer policy manuals. Ultimately, through a combination of our data matching and public records searches, we selected 15 case studies from 11 states. In addition, to the extent possible, we conducted searches to determine whether the sex offenders in our cases had previous criminal histories or were the subject of previous allegations of abuse. We also interviewed experts in fields related to child abuse investigations, prosecutions, and prevention.

To provide an overview of selected federal and state laws, we researched federal and state laws related to the employment of sex offenders in K-12 public and private schools. Specifically, we searched for prohibitions against working or being present in schools, requirements for conducting criminal history checks, other regulations pertaining to termination of employment or revocation of a teaching license, and requirements for mandatory reporting of suspected child abuse. Our analysis of relevant laws focused solely on statutory provisions at the state level because of their greater degree of permanence. We did not analyze state regulations or policies, nor any laws, regulations, or policies at the local or school district level. We performed our work from April 2010 to September 2010 in accordance with standards prescribed by the Council of the Inspectors General on Integrity and Efficiency.

CASES OF INDIVIDUALS WITH HISTORIES OF SEXUAL MISCONDUCT HIRED OR RETAINED BY PUBLIC AND PRIVATE SCHOOLS

Our 15 cases show that individuals with histories of sexual misconduct were hired or retained by public and private schools as teachers, administrative and support staff, volunteers, and contractors. In at least 11 of these 15 cases, schools allowed offenders with histories of targeting children to obtain or continue employment. Even more disturbing, in at least 6 of the cases, offenders used their new positions as school employees or volunteers to abuse more children after they were hired. We identified the following factors contributing to these employment actions.

Voluntary Separations and Positive Recommendations: In four of the cases we investigated, school officials allowed teachers who would have been subject to disciplinary action for sexual misconduct toward students to resign or otherwise separate from the school rather than face punishment. As a result, these teachers were able to truthfully inform prospective employers that they had never been fired from a teaching position and eventually were able to harm more children. In three of these four cases, school officials actually provided positive recommendations or reference letters for the teachers. We found that suspected abuse was not always reported to law enforcement or child protective services. Examples from our case studies include the following.

- An Ohio teacher was allowed to resign after a school investigation revealed he was having relationships with students that were "too much like boyfriend and girlfriend." However, district officials felt that they still did not have enough evidence to fire the teacher. Subsequently, the school superintendent wrote him a letter of

6 United States Government Accountability Office

recommendation, which the offender used to apply to a second Ohio school district, describing him as possessing "many qualities of an outstanding teacher." The school did not provide us with any evidence that this suspected abuse was reported to law enforcement or child protective services. The teacher was later convicted for committing sexual battery on a sixth grade girl at the second Ohio school district.

- A Connecticut public school district compelled a teacher to resign after he accessed pornography on a school computer. Although the school district reported the abuse to child protective services, a district administrator told another Connecticut school seeking a reference that they would rehire the teacher "without reservation." A second Connecticut school district also compelled him to resign, but his separation specifically directed all inquiries from future employers to the superintendent and agreed that he would provide a letter of recommendation. This school district also provided him with positive references. He was eventually hired by a third Connecticut school district, where he was convicted of sexually assaulting two students.

- A Louisiana private school district allowed a teacher's contract to expire after his eighth grade students searched his name on the Internet and discovered he was a registered sex offender. The school did not pursue action or notify authorities, but did provide him with a letter of recommendation, which he used to apply to another Louisiana school, which eventually hired him.[7] There, he is alleged to have engaged in inappropriate conversations with a student using an instant messaging service.

The school officials we interviewed cited a variety of reasons for allowing the resignations and providing the recommendations. One administrator told us that it could cost up to $100,000 to fire a teacher, even with "a slam dunk case." Other officials told us that, depending on the terms of a separation agreement, school administrators may not be able to provide anything less than a positive recommendation for an employee for fear of potential lawsuits. One expert we spoke with noted that it is often easier and faster for school administrators to remove a problem teacher informally in order to protect the children within their own district, especially when the administrator agrees to provide a positive recommendation to encourage a resignation.

Nonexistent Preemployment Criminal History Checks: In 10 of our 15 cases, school officials did not perform preemployment criminal history checks on prospective employees, including teachers, administrative staff, maintenance workers, volunteers, and contractors. As a result, registered sex offenders were allowed to gain access to both public and private schools. In 7 of these 10 cases, the offenders had been convicted for offenses against children and in at least 2 of the cases, they subsequently committed sexual crimes against children at the schools where they were working or volun-- teering. The documents we reviewed and the officials we spoke with indicated that the schools chose to forego these checks for a variety of reasons, including that they felt that the process was too time- consuming and costly or that the positions in question would not require daily interaction with children. We found that although the cost of performing a criminal history check varies by state, generally a fingerprint- based national and state check ranges from $21 to $99, paid by either the applicant or the school, and takes as long as 6 weeks to complete. Some schools also told us that they do not perform criminal history checks for support staff, such as maintenance workers, until after they have reported to work. Examples from our case studies including the following.

- An Arizona public school hired a teacher who had been convicted in Florida for lewd and lascivious acts with a minor. The school chose not to conduct a criminal history check on the teacher because it was in a hurry to fill the position. Ultimately, the offender was arrested and convicted for sexually abusing a young female student at the school.
- A church-run private school in Ohio employed a maintenance worker who had been convicted in California for lewd and lascivious acts with two minors. The school told us it did not conduct a criminal history check because the maintenance worker was supposed to work primarily for the church that operated the school. However, officials told us that he had regularly worked at the school and frequently interacted with the children, going so far as to buy them meals.
- In New York, a public school employed a maintenance worker for 5 months until the results of a criminal history check conducted after he had already reported to work revealed that he had been convicted of raping a woman at knife point and was classified as a threat to public safety.
- A Florida public school allowed an individual who was convicted of having sex with an underage male to work as a volunteer coach without a criminal history check, even though school policy provided

8   United States Government Accountability Office

that volunteers would be subject to such checks. He was eventually arrested for having sexual contact with a student on one of the school's sports teams.

As we previously noted, state laws with regard to employing sex offenders and conducting criminal history checks vary widely; see appendix I for an overview.

Inadequate Criminal History Checks: Even if schools do perform criminal history checks on employees, they may not be adequate because they are not national, fingerprint-based, or recurring. For example:

- Schools in eight of our cases told us that they conducted state criminal history checks, which only reveal offenses committed by a prospective employee in the state where it is conducted. These schools were located in California, Ohio, New York, Michigan, and Louisiana. Although we did not identify any cases where conducting a state criminal history check resulted in hiring an employee who committed an offense in another state, such an outcome is highly likely.
- We identified one school in Michigan that used a name-based criminal history search to hire an administrative employee. This online search required officials to search for the precise name under which an individual's criminal background is recorded. However, the officials used a common nickname instead of the applicant's full name, so the search did not reveal his eight convictions, which included various sex offenses. A fingerprint criminal history check would likely have revealed these charges.
- None of the schools we spoke with indicated that they perform recurring criminal history checks. In fact, only a few states have laws requiring schools to conduct such recurring checks intended to identify individuals if they commit offenses while they are employed at schools. For example, we identified two cases where sex offenders were currently employed by California public schools, despite the fact that California has a "subsequent arrest notifications" process to track the criminal history of employees after they are hired.[8] For example, one school never received a subsequent arrest notification when one of its maintenance workers was convicted of sexual battery in 1999. Since they conducted no recurring criminal history checks, school

officials were unaware of the employee's conviction until we notified them during the course of this investigation. In the other case, school officials received notice of an administrative employee's 2000 arrest for the molestation of a minor, but did not terminate his employment because they believed they were not legally obligated to do so. These officials subsequently left the school district and did not notify current staff about the arrest. Current officials told us they did not have any reason to examine the offender's employment file during their tenure. Consequently, these officials were not aware that they were employing a convicted sex offender until we notified them. A recurring background check would likely have alerted current staff to the offense.

Red Flags on Employment Applications: Many of the schools we spoke with require job applicants to self-report basic information regarding their criminal background, but in three of our cases, schools failed to ask applicants about troubling responses. For example, an applicant for an Arizona teaching position answered yes when asked if he had been convicted of "a dangerous crime against children." However, that school could provide no information to suggest that it followed up with the applicant or law enforcement about this admission before hiring the offender. The offender eventually was arrested for sexually abusing a young female student at the school. In the two remaining cases, applicants did not provide any response when asked about previous criminal history and school officials could not provide evidence that they had inquired about the discrepancy or required the applicant to provide the information. For example, a Michigan public school hired an administrative employee who had multiple convictions for sexual offenses. On his application, the offender did not respond to a question about whether he had ever been convicted of a crime, though he answered every other question on the application. Similarly, a California charter school hired an administrative employee who failed to answer a question about previous felony convictions, even though he had been convicted of a felony sex offense against a minor.

Table 1 provides a summary of the 15 cases we examined; a more detailed narrative on seven of the cases follows the table.

Table 1. Examples of Individuals with Histories of Sexual Misconduct Employed by K-1 2 Public, Private, and Charter Schools

Case	Location and type of facility, offender's occupation, and employment dates	Case details
1	• Multiple Ohio public schools • Teacher/Coach • August 1993 to May 2006	• An Ohio school district forced this teacher to resign after an investigation revealed his inappropriate conduct toward female students. • The school district provided a letter of recommendation for the teacher and he was hired at a neighboring district, where he was subsequently convicted for sexual battery against a sixth grade girl.
2	• California charter schools • Administrative employee • June 2007 to September 2008	• In 1998, the offender was convicted in California of a felony sexual offense against a minor. • The school did not perform a criminal history check of any kind on this offender due to resource constraints and because he was being hired as an administrative employee, not a teacher. • When asked on his job application whether he had ever been convicted of a felony, he did not answer; the school could not provide evidence that it had inquired into his failure to respond. • He was fired after a parent uncovered his criminal history through a search of the California public sex offender registry and notified the school. • The school now requires all prospective employees to undergo a fingerprint-based state criminal history check. However, this check will not reveal offenses committed in other states. California law requires all schools to conduct national fingerprint- based checks on employees.
3	• New York public school • Maintenance worker • July 2008 to November 2008	• In 1982, the offender was convicted in New York of raping a 21-year old woman at knifepoint behind a school; he was sentenced to 12 to 25 years in prison and classified as a level 3 sex offender, meaning that the offender is at high risk for repeat offenses and is a threat to public safety.

Case	Location and type of facility, offender's occupation, and employment dates	Case details
		• The school hired him "conditionally," meaning he was allowed to report to work prior to the completion of a state criminal history check. School officials told us they do not always perform these checks prior to employment because they considered the process both cost and time prohibitive. • The school fired the offender when the state criminal history check was completed; he was recently incarcerated for failure to comply with sex offender registration requirements.
4	• Illinois public school • Administrative employee • November 2007	• In 1992, the offender was convicted in Wisconsin of sexually assaulting a 9-year- old girl. • Through a series of contract arrangements, he was sent to a public school on a temporary basis as an administrative employee; alert administrative assistants called police when the offender was reluctant to sign the school's visitor log. • The offender failed to comply with an Illinois law that required him to report his employment status and work in schools to the police. • Neither the school nor any of the contractors responsible for his employment performed a criminal history check of any kind. • In January 2008, the offender pled guilty to multiple counts of Unlawful Presence within a School Zone.
6	• National school contractor • Two exam overseers • 2005 to 2009	• In May 1997, the first offender was convicted in California for multiple sex crimes against a child. • In July 2007, the second offender was convicted in California for engaging in lewd and lascivious acts with a child. • Both offenders were hired as exam overseers by testing center supervisors stationed at California public high schools (on behalf of a national contractor) without receiving a criminal history check. To our knowledge, they are no longer exam overseers in California.

Table 1. (Continued)

Case	Location and type of facility, offender's occupation, and employment dates	Case details
7	• California public school • Administrative employee • August 1998 to October 2010	• In 2000, the offender was convicted of misdemeanor sexual battery for restraining and molesting a minor. • The school was notified of his arrest and conviction by California police in 2000, but did not terminate his employment. The school was again notified of the offender's criminal history by GAO in July 2010. • After we notified the school of his criminal history and referred the case to the California Attorney General and California Department of Education, school officials placed the offender on administrative leave. He has since resigned.
8	• California public school • Maintenance worker • April 1985 to August 2010	• In 1999, the offender was convicted in California of misdemeanor sexual battery for groping a pregnant, blind woman. • The school never received notice of his sex offender status even though California has a subsequent arrest notification process for school employees. In addition, the offender lied in response to a question about his criminal background on a 2008 promotion application. • After we notified the school of his criminal history, school officials confronted the offender and he immediately resigned.
9	• Multiple Connecticut public schools • Teacher	• This offender was compelled to resign midyear from one Connecticut public school district for accessing pornography on his school computer. • This school provided a positive recommendation to another district, where the teacher continued to have disciplinary problems
	• August 2002 to December 2008	• He was again compelled to resign midyear; this school district also provided him with positive references. • While at yet another school, the teacher was arrested and convicted for sexually assaulting multiple underage female students.

Case	Location and type of facility, offender's occupation, and employment dates	Case details
10	• Ohio private school • Maintenance worker • June 2003 to June 2008	• In 1989, the offender was convicted in California for engaging in lewd and lascivious acts with two minors. • He moved to Ohio, where he was hired as a maintenance worker without receiving a criminal history check of any kind by a church which operated a private school. He provided custodial services regularly for the private school and interacted with children, going so far as to buy them meals. • His employment was terminated when he was arrested in June 2008 for failing to comply with sex offender registration requirements.
11	• Multiple schools in Maryland and Virginia • Teacher • November 2000 to March 2010	• Beginning in the early 1990s, this teacher is alleged to have engaged in a pattern of repeated abuses of underage students that he met through foreign exchange programs and school contacts. One Maryland public school, when faced with allegations of inappropriate conduct toward students, quietly allowed the teacher's contract to expire, rather then taking any disciplinary actions. The school later banned the teacher from school property. • At a Virginia public school, a parent provided school administrators with copies of inappropriate internet conversations; the school determined that since no laws were broken, there were no grounds to dismiss the teacher. • In July 2010, the offender pled guilty in Virginia to sexually abusing a 17-year-old student; he has been indicted on federal child pornography charges and is currently under investigation by North Carolina police for the alleged molestation of a 10-year-old disabled boy in 1978.

Table 1. (Continued)

Case	Location and type of facility, offender's occupation, and employment dates	Case details
12	• August 2001 to January 2002	• The Arizona school circumvented its normal hiring practices by allowing him to report to work as a teacher before the completion of a required fingerprint criminal history check, even though the offender had partially disclosed his criminal history on his application. • The school also failed to verify that he met basic job requirements: he had no state teaching certificate and his resume listed positions as a rental car worker, a lifeguard, and athletic trainer, but no history of classroom instruction. • After he began work, the offender failed to submit legible fingerprints for the background check, but the school never followed up to make sure his criminal history check was completed. • The school terminated his employment when he was arrested for inappropriate sexual contact with a young female student; an investigation revealed extensive sexual communiqués with the victim and video recordings of nude underage girls at a local pool.
13	• Louisiana private and public schools • Teacher • June 2006 to October 2007	• The offender was convicted on multiple counts of indecent exposure from 1989 to 1998, which led to the revocation of his Texas teaching certificate. • A Louisiana private school desperate to hire teachers in the aftermath of Hurricane Katrina allowed the offender to report to work without receiving a criminal history check. His contract was allowed to expire after his students discovered he was a sex offender, but no disciplinary actions were taken against him, and he was provided with a positive letter of recommendation. • A Louisiana public school hired him the day before the following school year started and again allowed him to report to work without a criminal history check. • He resigned after he was confronted with allegations that he had engaged in inappropriate sexual conversations with a student, for which he was charged with a second sex offense in 2007; a warrant is currently out for his arrest.

Case	Location and type of facility, offender's occupation, and employment dates	Case details
14	• Florida public school • Volunteer coach	• In 2008, the offender was convicted for engaging in consensual sex with an underage male.
	• Unknown to January 2009	• He worked as a volunteer coach for a Florida high school without receiving a criminal history check, even though school policy required such checks for volunteers. • He was arrested in 2009 for again having sex with an underage male, a member of one of the school's athletic teams who he had met through his coaching position. The charges are still pending and the offender is incarcerated while awaiting trial.
15	• California public school • Arts volunteer • October 2008 to January 2009	• Beginning in 1969, the offender was convicted of multiple sex offenses, including a felony conviction in 1999 for engaging in sex with two underage boys; police noted that he specifically targeted troubled youths. • He volunteered with a school arts program without receiving a criminal history check. School officials only learned of his criminal history when he was arrested in February 2009 for failing to comply with his sex offender registration requirements.

Source: Records including police reports, court documents, and interviews.

[a] A charter school is a public school that has been exempted from many of the statutes and regulations that apply to public school districts. The "charter," a license to operate, is granted by the local school district, county office of education, or state department of education.

Case 1: After being forced to resign from teaching at one Ohio public school system due to allegations of inappropriate relationships with female students, this offender received a letter of recommendation, and was hired to teach at a second Ohio public school district where he was later convicted of sexual battery against a student.

In August 1993, the offender began working at the first Ohio public school district as a teacher and also coached several sports. During his fourth year of teaching, an investigation confirmed that the teacher was acting inappropriately toward multiple female students. According to the summary of this investigation, the superintendent found that multiple coworkers agreed that the teacher's relationships with female students were "too much like

16 United States Government Accountability Office

boyfriend/girlfriend." Coworkers also noted that the teacher was found in a room with the lights off supposedly counseling a female student on more than one occasion and that he would become overly infatuated with a single girl each year. Further interviews with students, parents, and the teacher himself corroborated these allegations. For example, parents of the female athletes he coached agreed there was generally too much touching of the players. One student noted that a number of girls dropped out of his class because of the way he behaved around female students. When confronted with allegations that some of his behavior was inappropriate, the teacher responded that "the girls loved what [he] was doing." The school did not provide us with any evidence that this suspected abuse was reported to authorities.

According to the current superintendent, district officials did not feel they had enough evidence to terminate the teacher and therefore gave him 1 year to find a new job.[9] The teacher submitted his letter of resignation in April 1997, effective in July 1997.[10] Despite having requested his resignation, the former district superintendent provided the teacher with a letter of recommendation which noted that the teacher "exhibited many qualities of an outstanding teacher" and "has an outgoing personality which is an asset in this area of instruction." In contrast, the former superintendent also sent a letter directly to the teacher saying that the teacher was at least guilty of "poor judgment" and "behavior unbecoming a professional educator." Although we were unable to locate the former superintendent to ask why he wrote such conflicting letters, the current superintendent said he believed that the former superintendent feared that the teacher would file a lawsuit if he disclosed any incriminating information.

Two months after his resignation, the teacher used the letter of recommendation from the former superintendent to apply for a position as a teacher at a second Ohio public school district. The teacher worked at the second school for nearly a decade, until 2006, when he was indicted on two counts of sexual battery by the county prosecutor. This indictment alleged that, several years prior, he committed sexual battery on a sixth grade girl while in a position of authority and employed by a school. The detective who investigated the case said that the local police department found out about the sexual battery years after it occurred because the victim decided to come forward with the allegations. During the investigation, the police obtained undercover recordings where the teacher incriminated himself by describing sexual acts performed between him and the victim. According to the detective who investigated the sexual battery case, the second school district was never informed of any allegations of inappropriate conduct by the first school district. In May 2006, the teacher pled guilty to both counts of sexual battery and was sentenced to 2 years in state prison.

Case 7: This administrative employee was convicted of misdemeanor sexual battery while employed at a California public school district. Even though the school district was notified of his arrest and conviction by police in 2000 and by GAO in July 2010, district officials decided to retain him as an employee. After we referred this case to the California Attorney General and the California Department of Education, the school district placed this individual on administrative leave. He has since resigned.

In August 1998, this man was employed as an administrative employee in a California public school district. In February 2000, he molested a minor and the arresting officer charged the offender with a felony sex offense. In May 2000, a California court convicted him of misdemeanor sexual battery. The offender received a 120-day prison sentence and 3 years probation for the misdemeanor conviction and was required to register as a sex offender. Notes from the offender's personnel file at the school district indicate that he may have served his prison time using personal leave, which was known to school officials.

In March 2000, district officials were notified of the offender's arrest by police through California's subsequent arrest notification system, wherein the fingerprints a school employee submits during the hiring process are used to track any arrests occurring during his tenure as an employee. California law prohibits an individual convicted of an offense requiring registration as a sex offender from being hired or retained by a public school district. Once notified of the arrest, the offender's lawyer, former district personnel officials, and a consulting lawyer for the district met to discuss whether the district could fire the offender. The district ultimately decided to retain him. According to the consulting lawyer for the district, the district believed that the offender's continued employment was "within the letter and intent of California law."

In July 2010, we notified current district personnel officials that an administrative employee in their school system was in fact a registered sex offender. When we asked why he had been allowed to retain his position, a current district personnel official stated that no district officials were aware of his sex offender status, even though his employment file contained documentation on the arrest, charges, and conviction, as well as notes from the March 2000 discussion. The personnel officials explained to us that they did not have any reason to examine the offender's employment file during their tenure. District officials stated that while all new applicants to the district are

18 United States Government Accountability Office

subject to a state criminal history check (including submission of fingerprints to the California Department of Justice), existing employees are not subject to recurring criminal history checks. Had a recurring criminal history check been performed, current personnel officials may have been made aware of the offender's conviction. According to a current district personnel official, improved information sharing between former and current district personnel officials would have increased the likelihood of the school district taking appropriate action to safeguard students from the offender. In addition, while the offender had been registering his school employment with the local police in accordance with his sex offender registration requirements, police did not inform the school after the original subsequent arrest notification. After we referred this case to the California Attorney General and the California Department of Education, the school district placed this individual on administrative leave. He has since resigned.

Case 8: This maintenance worker was convicted of misdemeanor sexual battery while employed by a California public school district. Since the district did not perform any recurring criminal history checks, district officials remained unaware of his conviction until we notified them. After this notification, district officials immediately confronted the offender, who resigned.

In April 1985, this offender began employment in a California public school district as a maintenance worker. After he was hired, the offender groped a pregnant, blind woman and was subsequently convicted in California in 1999 for misdemeanor sexual battery.[11] He received a 120-day prison sentence and 3 years probation, and was required to register as a sex offender. The offender later told school officials that he had served his prison sentence while on leave from the school district for a work-related injury. In 2009, the offender was promoted after over 2 decades of service in the same California public school district. On his promotion application, the offender falsely stated he was never convicted of a misdemeanor or felony.

In July 2010, we notified school officials that this individual was currently employed in their district even though the California Education Code prohibits individuals convicted of sexual battery from retaining employment in California public schools. District officials then confronted the offender, who resigned immediately. Though the offender's employment had continued for over a decade after his conviction, the officials told us that they were not aware of his status as a sex offender, despite California's subsequent arrest notification process. The human resource official responsible for receiving subsequent arrest notifications confirmed that the offender had passed a fingerprint criminal history check when he was hired. Even though the offender's fingerprints should have been on file, the district did not receive any notifications from California police about his conviction. In addition, district officials told us that school employees are not subject to recurring criminal history checks and confirmed that no documentation of the offender's arrest or conviction existed in district records. District officials also told us that the offender had work-related injuries requiring absences from work. At the time of his resignation, the offender told school officials that one of those absences coincided with his prison term.

We were unable to determine why the subsequent arrest notification process failed. However, a police officer involved with the maintenance worker stated that he had registered as a sex offender in accordance with annual requirements since his conviction. The officer, who just began working with sex offenders in 2010, noted that the offender correctly reported to law enforcement that he was currently employed by the California public school district. However, the officer stated that he did not question the offender further on his employment during their meetings even though California prohibits sex offenders from being employed at schools. The officer stated that he had no reason to believe the offender was inappropriately employed because the offender had been working in the California school district during each of the 12 years he had registered as a sex offender.

Case 9: After being compelled to resign from teaching in two Connecticut school districts—due to accessing pornography on school computers at one district and for "performance reasons" at the other—this offender received positive recommendations from both districts and was hired to teach at another Connecticut school district, where he was convicted of sexual assault against two students.

In early December 2003, a Connecticut public school district compelled a teacher to resign in the middle of his second year of teaching for accessing pornography on school computers. In mid-November, the school district had placed the teacher on paid administrative leave pending an investigation into allegations that his computer was used to access pornographic Web sites. According to one district official, the teacher claimed that he had allowed students to access his computer account, and that the students had accessed the pornographic Web sites. The school reported the potential child abuse to state authorities for investigation, but before taking further disciplinary action, the school district reached a separation agreement with the teacher. This agreement was signed by the school district, the teacher, and the local teachers' union, and required the teacher to unconditionally resign. The agreement also required the teacher to waive all rights to file any claim against the school district related to his employment or separation from employment. The agreement did not contain a confidentiality or nondisclosure clause. The teacher submitted a letter of resignation stating that his separation was for "personal reasons," effective December 2003.

Beginning in January 2004, the teacher worked as a substitute teacher in a nearby school district, where he worked for the remainder of the school year, until obtaining a permanent position as a teacher in a third Connecticut school district in July. The application for teaching in this school district required the teacher to provide his employment background with employment dates, but did not ask for reasons for leaving any previous jobs. Although the school district did not require any references, the teacher submitted three letters of recommendation. One of those recommendations came from an administrator of the district which had forced the teacher's resignation in December 2003 and was dated 1 week after the separation agreement was finalized. When we asked the district's legal counsel why the administrator provided a positive recommendation, he told us that the administrator claimed that she was unaware of the reason for the teacher's resignation and that she was only providing a positive recommendation regarding his classroom performance.

In March 2007, the teacher again submitted a midyear resignation letter, although he taught through the end of that school year. According to one school district official involved in the process, the teacher's resignation was requested for "performance reasons." The school district and the teacher signed a confidential memorandum of understanding outlining the terms of the teacher's resignation: the teacher would submit an irrevocable letter of resignation effective at the end of the school year stating "personal reasons." The memorandum of understanding further stipulated that all requests for information regarding the teacher would be directed to the superintendent and that the superintendent alone would be allowed to provide references for the teacher.

Despite the compelled departure from two school districts, in July 2007 the teacher received positive recommendations from both school districts when he applied for and obtained a similar teaching position at a high school in a fourth Connecticut school district. On the application that the teacher submitted for this job, when asked whether he had ever been fired by an employer or told he would be fired if he did not resign, the teacher responded "No." As requested, the teacher submitted three references, all of which were from the most recent school district where he had worked.12 School officials told us that because the three submitted references only covered one of the two school districts listed as prior employers in the teacher's application, they contacted the other district and spoke to an administrator to receive an additional reference. All four references—including the administrator from the district which forced the teacher's resignation for accessing pornography— gave positive reviews of the teacher and stated that they would rehire him without reservation. According to one school official involved in the hiring process, the principal of the school from which the teacher was forced to resign for accessing pornography only stated that the teacher left his job because of "family issues and personal problems." The same official told us that had the school known about the teacher's forced resignations, it would have hired another candidate.

In December 2008, during his second year at his new position in the fourth Connecticut school district, the teacher again resigned in the middle of the school year for "personal reasons," this time when confronted by school administrators with allegations of having an inappropriate relationship with a 17-year-old student. At the time of his resignation, the teacher admitted to kissing the student. According to the superintendent, the district intended to suspend the teacher but was preempted by the teacher's immediate voluntary resignation. The superintendent did request that the state Board of Education revoke the teacher's certification.[13] A subsequent investigation conducted by the police and the Department of Child and Family Services revealed that the teacher had intimate relations with two students, including sexual intercourse in the school's auditorium. In 2009, he pled guilty to two counts of second degree sexual assault, was sentenced to 7 years in prison and 20 years probation, and required to register as a sex offender.

Case 11: Despite allegedly engaging in a pattern of repeated sexual abuse of underage male students, this offender taught at several schools in Maryland and Virginia before recently pleading guilty to sexually abusing an underage student at a Virginia public school at which he taught. He is currently under investigation by state and federal authorities for numerous offenses dating back to 1978 and was indicted by a grand jury on multiple federal child pornography charges.

The offender's pattern of abuse against students began in the early 1990s. At that time, he was teaching English to students in Japan. In 1994, the offender accompanied an underage Japanese student on a trip to the United States for several weeks. The offender allegedly provided the student with

22   United States Government Accountability Office

sufficient alcohol to cause unconsciousness and then sexually abused him, as evidenced by video recordings and photographs kept by the offender. In 1999, after returning to the United States, the offender hosted an underage Danish exchange student who, during his stay, found pictures in the offender's possession which indicated that the offender had abused him. According to the student, after a confrontation, the offender apologized and burned the photos, but investigators recently found copies of the photos remaining in the offender's possession. At the time, the offender confided in someone regarding this incident, who subsequently contacted police. At the offender's urging, the exchange student told police that nothing improper had happened. Based on the student's statements, police discontinued the investigation.

In November 2000, a public school district in Maryland hired the offender as a teacher. In 2002, the parents of a district student contacted the offender directly to request that he stop calling their son because they felt the contacts were inappropriate. While the parents did not contact the school district directly, rumors about inappropriate relationships reached the school board and the alleged inappropriate contact was a discussion point as the district was deciding whether to keep the teacher or quietly allow his contract to expire. We do not know whether school officials contacted local law enforcement about their suspicions. In June 2003, the offender's contract with the district was allowed to expire. The district also banned the offender from district property.

In September 2003, the offender began hosting an underage German exchange student. The foreign exchange company received complaints of threatening behavior about the offender from the exchange student and removed the student from the offender's home immediately, with the help of local police. In May 2004, the student sought a restraining order against the offender, but the judge stated that the harassment described was not grounds for a restraining order and denied the request. The offender is alleged to have sexually abused this exchange student, again evidenced by videos, photographs, and other mementos kept by the offender.

In August 2007, the offender began teaching in a Virginia public school district using multiple positive letters of recommendation as references. In September 2008, a concerned parent confronted the offender about inappropriate conversations with two underage boys (her son and a friend) through a networking Web site. The parent also provided copies of the inappropriate conversations to the school's administration. The school's principal spoke to the offender and told him not to have any contact with the two boys. The principal, in consultation with lawyers, a school human resource officer, and local police, determined that since no laws had been broken, the school had no grounds to dismiss the offender, despite the evidence provided by the parent.

In February 2010, an underage student alleged that the offender provided him with alcohol and engaged in inappropriate sexual contact. The offender was arrested in February 2010 on felony charges for sex offenses involving a minor. He pled guilty to these charges and was sentenced to 1 year in prison in October 2010. During the investigation of this case, law enforcement officials discovered extensive evidence of sexual abuse of numerous unidentified underage males, including handwritten recollections, homemade videos, and photographs. He has been charged by federal authorities with numerous counts of possession of child pornography and transporting it across state lines. In addition, North Carolina police are currently investigating the alleged molestation of a 10- year-old disabled boy at the offender's family home in 1978.

Case 12: This offender was convicted of sexually assaulting a minor in Florida and subsequently worked as a teacher in a school in Arizona for 6 months without having his criminal history or educational qualifications verified by the school district.

In March 1994, the offender was convicted in Florida of lewd and lascivious assault against a victim under the age of 16. The offender was given probation but was imprisoned for a violation from July 1996 to June 1999. Once released, he was required to register as a sex offender permanently. He moved to Arizona in 2001. In August 2001, an Arizona school district hired the offender as a teacher. On his application for the position, the offender was asked several questions regarding his criminal history, and he correctly responded that he had been convicted of "a dangerous crime against children," but failed to provide the complete details of his conviction, as the application required. When we asked the school how they had responded to this disclosure, they were unable to provide any information to suggest that they had independently verified any of the offender's responses or requested the missing details of his conviction. In addition, his resume listed an employment history including positions as a rental car worker, a lifeguard, and athletic trainer, but no history of classroom instruction. The teaching position he held also required a teaching certificate, but there is no documentation from the school to show that the offender received or submitted such a certificate.

In addition to failing to verify his educational requirements, the school district neglected to conduct a criminal history check on the offender. Arizona requires criminal history checks for all public school employees. To complete the check, the applicant must turn in his/her fingerprints to the Arizona Department of Public Safety (DPS), which performs a state and federal criminal history check. Once the Arizona DPS completes the criminal history check and verifies that the applicant is suitable for school work, a fingerprint clearance card is issued, which the applicant must then send to the Arizona Department of Education. According to school officials, this process can take up to 90 days. In this case, the school district circumvented this requirement because it was anxious to fill the position before school started. Instead of treating the offender as an employee applying for a teaching position, the school district treated him as though he were applying for a nonteaching position, such as a food service worker or a bus driver.14 The school district performed a verbal reference check, and allowed the offender to provide a fingerprint clearance card at a later date. The district's verbal reference check involved contacting employment references, provided by the applicant, and asking questions such as, "Has this applicant ever sexually abused a minor?" In this case, the offender provided references who gave glowing recommendations.

As requested by the school, the offender eventually sent fingerprints to the Arizona DPS, but the Arizona DPS sent back a letter several months later stating that the fingerprint criminal history check could not be completed because the submitted fingerprints were smudged. A message was placed in the offender's personnel file noting the need for him to complete the fingerprint criminal history check, but there was no indication of any additional follow-up by school officials on the subject.

In January 2002, the offender was arrested for sexually abusing a young female student between December 2001 and January 2002. The offender was alleged to have touched the girl at the school and to have sent the girl sexually explicit letters. Officers investigating the case found multiple letters between the offender and the girl containing mature sexual content, some in a gym bag the offender was carrying at the time of his arrest. Police also found a home video recording of girls changing into bathing suits and walking around naked in a restroom. The offender could be heard adjusting the camera and talking on this video, which the Arizona police suspected was shot at a pool where the offender had previously worked as a manager.

The offender was found guilty of felony sexual abuse and luring a minor for sexual exploitation in 2002. He was sentenced to 4 years in prison, as well as 15 years probation. In 2010, he was convicted for failing to register as a sex offender as required. He was sentenced to 12 years in prison, and is currently incarcerated.

Case 13: In June 1998, this man was convicted for the second time for misdemeanor indecent exposure and was required to register as a sex offender. He was a teacher in Texas at the time, and remained there until May 2001, when his teaching certification was permanently revoked for engaging in a pattern of sexually inappropriate behavior. At least two schools in Louisiana, one private and one public, subsequently hired him without conducting criminal history checks. He continued to teach at the public school until October 2007, when he voluntarily resigned after being accused of having inappropriate sexual conversations with students.

With the loss of his Texas teaching license in 2001, the offender taught in Mexico temporarily then moved to Louisiana. According to his resume, he worked at a series of Louisiana public and private schools from August 2002 until June 2006; we were unable to verify the circumstances leading to this employment. In June 2006, he was hired by a high school in a Louisiana private school district. The principal mistakenly assumed he had received a Louisiana criminal history check from a prior Louisiana school, and, desperate to hire teachers in the aftermath of Hurricane Katrina, allowed the offender to report to work without conducting a criminal history check. The principal did, however, contact a Louisiana private school that was listed as a previous employer for an oral reference, and the offender was highly recommended. He worked for 1 year on a year-to- year contract before eighth grade students identified him as a sex offender after conducting an Internet search for photos of him for a school event. His contract was allowed to expire, but no disciplinary actions were taken against him and we found no evidence that the school contacted law enforcement to report the offender's presence in the school. After the expiration of this contract, the principal contacted the private school that had provided a positive reference for the offender to determine why she had not been provided with information on the offender's past. The private school officials she spoke with stated that the specific individual who had provided the reference was a close friend of the offender, and that no one else at the private school would have provided a positive reference.

The day before the beginning of the 2007-2008 school year, a principal from a Louisiana public high school hired the offender to begin immediately teaching, based on a resume appearing on an online job search Web site for prospective teachers. Because the hire occurred so close to the beginning of the school year, school officials told us they did not complete a state criminal history and reference checks before the offender reported for duty. School officials told us that, at that time, completing the state fingerprint background check generally took between 3 and 6 months.[15]

In his application to work for the school, the offender falsely stated that he had not been convicted of a criminal offense and that he held or was eligible for a teaching certificate in Texas. The offender further indicated that he was in the process of applying for a Louisiana teaching certificate; however, the Louisiana teacher certification database holds no record of the offender. He also provided a letter of recommendation from the principal of the private school that had allowed his contract to expire in 2007. When we spoke to the principal regarding this recommendation, she told us that she had never personally provided a positive reference for the offender, but that a subordinate may have drafted the letter in her absence.

A few months into the school year, a parent of one of the students provided the principal with copies of inappropriate sexual conversations between the offender and a student over an instant messaging service. The school district began investigating the allegations and became aware of the offender's criminal history. The superintendent of the district told us that he intended to take action against the teacher, but was preempted by the teacher's immediate voluntary resignation. Police were notified of the allegations, which resulted in November 2007 charges of indecent behavior with a minor and failing to fulfill sex offender registration requirements. A warrant is currently out for his arrest on these charges.

OVERVIEW OF FEDERAL AND STATE LAWS RELATED TO THE EMPLOYMENT OF SEX OFFENDERS IN K-12 PUBLIC AND PRIVATE SCHOOLS

We found no federal laws regulating the employment of sex offenders in public or private schools and widely divergent laws at the state level, especially with regard to requirements and methods for conducting criminal history checks on employees. For a summary of laws related to the hire and retention of sex offenders by schools in all 50 states and the District of Columbia, see appendix 1.

Federal law: The Adam Walsh Child Protection and Safety Act of 2006 requires the Department of Justice to conduct a criminal history check for employees who work around children at the request of a public or private school. This check allows for a fingerprint-based criminal history search of the Federal Bureau of Investigation's National Crime Information Center database. However, federal law does not require schools to use this service. In addition, we found no federal laws that restrict the employment of sex offenders in public or private schools or that mandate criminal history checks for employees at these schools.

Prohibitions working in or being present at schools: A majority of states have enacted laws to restrict sex offenders from having access to schools, but they may only apply to select types of schools (e.g., public schools) in certain situations. Eighteen states have broad restrictions prohibiting registered sex offenders from entering, or being a specified distance from, all schools.[16] Seventeen states have some type of statute that specifically prohibits registered sex offenders from working or volunteering at or near schools.[17] However, in some states such prohibitions may only apply to individuals who have been convicted of a felony.

Criminal history check requirements for public and private school employees: These requirements vary widely. For example, 2 states do not appear to have any laws requiring criminal history checks for either public or private school employees.[18] Twenty-five states and the District of Columbia require criminal history checks for all public school employees.[19] Six states require criminal history checks for all public school employees and conditional checks for private school employees, often tied to such things as accreditation or acceptance of state scholarship funds.[20] Seven states require that both public and private school employees undergo criminal history checks.[21] The remaining 10 states require checks only for select employees in certain situations. For example:

- Four states require criminal history checks for licensed teachers, but make no reference to other types of employees.[22]
- Four states require checks for employees only if they have unsupervised or direct contact with children.[23]
- One state only requires criminal history checks for certified teachers and administrators if they have not been residents in the state for 5 years.[24]
- One state requires individual public school districts to have a policy which determines which employees are subject to criminal history checks.[25]

28 United States Government Accountability Office

Criminal history check requirements for contractors and volunteers: Only five states require criminal history checks for all contractors at both public and private schools.[26] Seven states require criminal history checks for all contractors at public schools only.[27] Other states require criminal history checks for contractors only under select circumstances, typically if they have direct access to children. Only eight states require criminal history checks for those volunteering with children.[28]

Method of conducting criminal history checks: As shown in appendix I, the vast majority of states specify that teacher and school employee criminal history checks are to be fingerprint-based and must check both national and state databases. However, not all states specifically require that criminal history checks be completed prior to an employee's start date. In addition, two states[29] limit the check to state databases, while another state limits the check to state databases if the employee or applicant has been a state resident for the prior 2 years.[30] In addition, some states specify that criminal history checks must be reperformed at specified intervals[31] and some states rely upon a system of subsequent conviction or arrest notifications,[32] but often such systems only catch subsequent convictions or arrests in the same state and may miss such events that occur in other states.

Termination of employment, revocation of license, or refusal to hire: Some states prohibit public schools from employing an individual convicted of a violent or sexual felony,[33] while others have a broader prohibition that applies to both public and private schools, as well as to contractors and employees.[34] Other states apply such mandatory disqualification criteria only to holders of teaching licenses or certificates.[35]

Requirements to report suspected child abuse: All 50 states and the District of Columbia have statutes that mandate that teachers and other school officials report suspected child abuse, including sexual abuse, to law enforcement, child protection agencies, or both. Typically, these statutes require the teacher or official to have a reasonable suspicion that abuse occurred before making such a report. Although these statutes were developed with the goal of preventing abuse by parents or guardians, they also cover abuse by a teacher or school employee. Furthermore, several states have adopted additional statutory precautions to ensure that abuse allegations against school employees are not suppressed by school officials; however, at least half of the states do not have any such additional statutory precautions.

These statutes vary widely across the states and require mandatory reporting such as

- superintendents must report to the state education department or licensing board the resignation or dismissal of a licensed educator following reports of alleged abuse;
- superintendents must report to law enforcement crimes, including sexual abuse, committed on school property; and
- prosecutors must report to the state education department or licensing board felony convictions of licensed educators.

As agreed with your offices, unless you publicly announce the contents of this report earlier, we plan no further distribution until 10 days from the report date. At that time, we will send copies of this report to relevant congressional committees, the Department of Education, and the Department of Justice. In addition, this report will be available at no charge on GAO's Web site at www.gao.gov.

For further information about this report, please contact me at (202) 512-6722 or kutzg@gao.gov. Contact points for our Offices of Congressional Relations and Public Affairs may be found on the last page of this report.

Sincerely yours,

Gregory D. Kutz
Managing Director
Forensic Audits and Special Investigations

APPENDIX I. SUMMARY OF STATE LAWS RELATED TO THE HIRING AND RETENTION OF SEX OFFENDERS

State	Prohibitions on sex offenders working in or being present at schools	Criminal history check requirements for school employees, contractors, and volunteers	Offenses requiring mandatory termination of employment or revocation of license	Mandatory reporting requirements
AL	Convicted sex offenders may not be employed within 500 feet of a school.	Public and private schools are required to conduct fingerprint-based FBI and state criminal history checks of employees with unsupervised access to children.	Individuals convicted of crimes involving the physical or mental injury, sexual abuse or exploitation, or maltreatment of a child are deemed unsuitable for employment.	All teachers and school officials must report known or suspected cases of child abuse or neglect to a duly constituted authority. If the report is received by the Department of Human Resources, it must report it to law enforcement.
AK	None located.	Teachers are required to undergo a fingerprint-based national criminal history check as part of the certification process. School bus drivers must undergo a fingerprint-based national criminal history check.	Individuals with a sex offense conviction may not hold a teacher certificate or a school bus driver license.	All public and private school teachers and employees are required to report to the Department of Health and Social Services when they suspect that a child has suffered abuse or neglect. Law enforcement who receive a report of abuse by a teacher are required to report the fact to the Professional Teaching Practices Commission.

State	Prohibitions on sex offenders working in or being present at schools	Criminal history check requirements for school employees, contractors, and volunteers	Offenses requiring mandatory termination of employment or revocation of license	Mandatory reporting requirements
AZ	None located.	Fingerprint-based federal and state criminal history checks are required of all certified teachers, public school employees, public school volunteers with unsupervised acces to children, and employees of public school contractors, and vendors.	Teachers convicted of sex offenses are subject to mandatory permanent revocation of their teaching certificate.	Licensed educators and school boards must report all reasonable allegations of misconduct by a licensed educator involving minors to the AZ Department of Education. All school personnel who reasonably believe that a child has been the victim of abuse must report to law enforcement or child protective services.
AR	Registered sex offenders may not enter the campus of a public school.	Teachers are required to undergo fingerprint-based national and state criminal history checks as part of the licensing and renewal processes. School districts must conduct a fingerprint –based national and state criminal history check of all nonlicensed employees.	Individuals with a felony or sex offense conviction may not hold a teacher license or be employed by a public school.	Public school superintendents must report to the Board of Education any employee who is convicted of a felony or certain misdemeanors or who is the subject of a substantiated report in the Child altreatment Central Registry. School teachers and officials must notify the Child Abuse Hotline if they have reasonable cause to suspect a child has been subject to abuse.
CA	Registered sex offenders may not be an employer, employee, contractor, or volunteer in positions that involve working with children.	Fingerprint-based national and state criminal history checks are required for all certified teachers, public and private school employees, and public and private school contract employees who may have contact with pupils.	Public schools may not employ persons convicted of sex offen-ses or violent or serious felonies. Individuals with a sex offense or violent or serious felony convic-tion may not hold a teacher certificate. Private schools must notify all parents before hiring a convicted sex offender.	If a licensed educator is dismissed, suspended, placed on administrative leave, or resigns as a result of or while an allegation of misconduct is pending, the school must report the allegation to the Committee on Credentials. All public and private school employees must notify law enforcement or the county welfare agency if they know or reasonably suspect a child has been the victim of abuse or neglect.

State	Prohibitions on sex offenders working in or being present at schools	Criminal history check requirements for school employees, contractors, and volunteers	Offenses requiring mandatory termination of employment or revocation of license	Mandatory reporting requirements
CO	None located.	Fingerprint-based national and state criminal history checks and previous employer checks are required of all public school teachers. Fingerprint-based national and state criminal history checks are required of all public school employees. Private schools are authorized to conduct fingerprint-based national and state criminal history checks of their employees.	Public and charter schools may not employ anyone with a felony or sexual offense conviction.	If a public school employee is dismissed or resigns as a result of an allegation of unlawful behavior involving a child, the school district must notify the CO Department of Education. Any public or private school employee who has reasonable cause to know or suspect that a child has been subjected to abuse or neglect must notify law enforcement or the county human services department.
CT	None located.	Fingerprint-based national and state criminal history checks are required of all public school employees. Private schools are authorized to conduct fingerprint- based national and state criminal history checks.	A conviction for child abuse or neglect or other selected serious felonies is grounds for revocation of a teaching certificate.	Prosecutors must notify the Commissioner of Education if a licensed educator is convicted of a felony. School teachers and officials who have reasonable cause to suspect a child has been abused or neglected must notify the Commissioner of Children and Families or law enforcement.

State	Prohibitions on sex offenders working in or being present at schools	Criminal history check requirements for school employees, contractors, and volunteers	Offenses requiring mandatory termination of employment or revocation of license	Mandatory reporting requirements
DE	Registered sex offenders may not loiter within 500 feet of a school.	Fingerprint-based FBI and state criminal history checks are required of all public school employees, school bus drivers, and public school student teachers, drivers, and public school student teachers.	A felony or child-victim conviction disqualifies an applicant from public school Employment or a school bus license.	Public and charter schools must report to the DE Secretary of Education when a licensed educator is dismissed, resigns, or retires following allegations of misconduct. Any school employee who knows or in good faith suspects child abuse or neglect shall notify the Department of Services for Children, Youth and Their Families.
DC	None located.	Periodic fingerprint-based local and FBI criminal history checks are required of all employees and volunteers in city organizations that provide services to children.	None located.	School teachers and officials who know or have reasonable cause to suspect child abuse or neglect must notify law enforcement or the Child and Family Services Agency.
FL	Sex offenders on supervised release whose victims were minors may not work or volunteer at any school.	Periodic (every 5 years) fingerprint-based FBI and state criminal history checks are required of all public school teachers and employees and contractual employees who have direct contact with students or are permitted access to school grounds when students are present. Private school owners or operators are required to undergo a fingerprint –based criminal history check and are	Individuals with a felony conviction or a misdemeanor conviction involveing a child are prohibited from employment in a public school or a private school that accepts state scholarships if they will have contact with children. Owners or operators of private schools may not have been convicted of a felony involving moral turpitude.	Public, charter schools, and private schools that accept state scholarships must notify the FL Department of Education after receipt of allegations of misconduct against a licensed educator. School personnel must notify the state hotline if they know or have reasonable cause to suspect child abuse.

State	Prohibitions on sex offenders working in or being present at schools	Criminal history check requirements for school employees, contractors, and volunteers	Offenses requiring mandatory termination of employment or revocation of license	Mandatory reporting requirements
GA	Registered sex offenders may not be employed by or volunteer at any school.	Fingerprint-based state and federal criminal history checks are required of all certified teachers and all public school employees.	None located.	Superintendents must report to the county board of education when an educator commits a sexual offense. School teachers and administrators with reasonable cause to believe that a child is a victim of abuse must notify a child welfare agency.
HI	None located.	Fingerprint-based FBI and state criminal history checks are required of all public and private school employees whose position places them in close proximity to children.	Conviction of a sexual offense is grounds for permanent revocation of a teaching license.	Employees or officers of any public or private school must notify law enforcement or the HI Department of Human Services if they have reason to believe that child abuse or neglect has occurred.
ID	Registered sex offenders may not enter school buildings or grounds or be involved in any school activity.	Fingerprint-based FBI and state criminal background and sex offender registry checks are required of all certified teachers, and public school employees with unsupervised contact with children. Private schools are authorized to conduct such checks of their employees.	Convicted felons may not receive a teaching certificate.	School districts must notify the ID State Department of Education when an educator is dismissed or resigns for a reason that could constitute grounds for certificate revocation. Teachers with reason to believe that a child has been abused or neglected must notivy law enforcement or the ID Deartment of Health & Welfare.

State	Prohibitions on sex offenders working in or being present at schools	Criminal history check requirements for school employees, contractors, and volunteers	Offenses requiring mandatory termination of employment or revocation of license	Mandatory reporting requirements
IL	Registered sex offenders may not be employed by or volunteer at any facility providing programs or services to children. Registered sex offenders may not be present within 500 feet of a school.	Fingerprint-based FBI and state criminal background and sex offender registry checks are required of all public school employees and employees of contractors (including school bus operators). In order to obtain state recognition, a private school must conduct such checks on its employees.	Felons convicted of sexual or physical abuse of a minor may not be employed by a public school. Felons are ineligible for a school bus license.	Superintendents must notify the State Superintendent of Education when any licensed educator is dismissed or resigns as a result of child abuse or neglect. School administrators and employees must notify the Department of Children & Family Services if they have reasonable cause to believe a child is abused or neglected.
IN	Persons convicted of sexually violent offenses or offenses against children may not work or volunteer on school property.	Fingerprint-based FBI and state criminal background and sex offender registry checks are required of all public, charter, and accredited private school employees and contractor employees.	Schools may not employ or contract with individuals convicted of violent or sexual felonies.	Public and private school employees who have reason to believe that a child has been ab-used or neglected must report the incident to law enforcement or the Department of Child Services.
IA	Registered sex offenders whose victims were minors may not be	Fingerprint-based FBI and state criminal background and sex offender registry checks are required of all public	Conviction of a crime related to the teaching profession is grounds for revocation of a teaching license. Conviction	Public and private schools must report to the state education board if a licensed educator is terminated or resigns as a result of alleged or actual misconduct.
	employed by, volunteer at, or serve as a contractor for a school.	school teachers.	of sex with a minor disqualifies an individual from holding a school bus license.	Licensed educators must report child abuse to the IA Department of Human Services.

Appendix I. (Continued

State	Prohibitions on sex offenders working in or being present at schools	Criminal history check requirements for school employees, contractors, and volunteers	Offenses requiring mandatory termination of employment or revocation of license	Mandatory reporting requirements
KS	None located.	None located.	Conviction of a violent, sexual, or child-victim offense disqualifies a teacher from receiving or renewing a teaching certificate.	School employees who have reason to suspect that a child has been harmed as a result of physical, mental, or emotional abuse or neglect or sexual abuse must notify the Department of Social & Rehabilitation Services.
KY	Registered sex offenders may not enter school property without advance permission of the principal or school board.	Fingerprint-based FBI and state criminal history checks are required of all public school teachers, student teachers, and employees. Public schools are authorized to conduct such a check of contractor employees, volunteers, and visitors. Private schools are authorized to conduct such checks of their employees.	Public schools may not employ individuals convicted of a sex offense felony.	Principals must report all sexual offenses that occur on school property to law enforcement. School personnel who have reasonable cause to believe that a child is neglected or abused must notify law enforcement.

State	Prohibitions on sex offenders working in or being present at schools	Criminal history check requirements for school employees, contractors, and volunteers	Offenses requiring mandatory termination of employment or revocation of license	Mandatory reporting requirements
LA	Persons convicted of sexually violent offenses may not be present on school property without permission. Persons convicted of sexual offenses against victims under 13 may not be present within 1000 feet of a school without permission. Persons Convicted of sexual offenses whose victims were minors may not be given parole or probation unless a condition of release is a prohibition on volunteering or working in a position that involves contact with children.	Fingerprint-based FBI and state criminal history checks are required of all public school employees and contractor employees.	Public and private schools may not employ or contract with an entity that employs individ-uals convicted of a violent or sexual felony if such individuals will have contact with students.	Public or private school personnel who have cause to believe that a child's physical or mental health or welfare is endangered as a result of abuse or neglect must notify law enforcement or child protective services.

State	Prohibitions on sex offenders working in or being present at schools	Criminal history check requirements for school employees, contractors, and volunteers	Offenses requiring mandatory termination of employment or revocation of license	Mandatory reporting requirements
ME	Convicted sex offenders whose victims were under 14 may not initiate contact with a child under 14 on school property.	Fingerprint-based national and state criminal history checks are required of all public school employees.	None located.	Teachers and school officials who know or have reasonable cause to suspect that a child has been abused or neglected must notify the district attorney.
MD	Registered sex offenders may not enter school property.	Fingerprint-based national and state criminal history checks are required of all public and private school employees.	Public or private schools may not employ an individual convicted of a violent felony or of child sexual abuse.	All educators who have reason to believe that a child has been subjected to abuse must notify law enforcement or the Department of Human Resources.
MA	The commissioner of probation must establish exclusion zones for persons on probation for sexually violent offenses or offenses against children to minimize contact with children.	Criminal history checks are required every 3 years of all public and accredited private school employees, volunteers, bus drivers, and contractor employees.	None located.	Public and private school teachers and administrators who have reason-able cause to believe that a child is suffering physical or emotional injury resulting from abuse must notify the Department of Social Services.

State	Prohibitions on sex offenders working in or being present at schools	Criminal history check requirements for school employees, contractors, and volunteers	Offenses requiring mandatory termination of employment or revocation of license	Mandatory reporting requirements
MI	Registered sex offenders may not work or loiter within 1000 feet of school property.	Fingerprint-based FBI and state criminal background and previous employer checks are private school employees, equired of all public and contractor employees, and bus drivers	Convicted sex offenders may not be employed in public or private schools.	School teachers and administrators must report suspected child abuse or neglect to the Department of Human Services.
MN	None located.	State criminal history checks are required of all public employees and volunteers. Public schools are authorized to conduct such checks on independent contractors. School bus licenses require a criminal history check.	Public schools may not employ an individual with a conviction for a violent or sexual felony.	School boards must report to the state Board of Teaching when a teacher or administrator is dismissed or resigns as a result of commission of a felony or immoral conduct. Educational professionals who know or have reason to believe a child is being neglected or physically or sexually abused must notify law enforcement or the local welfare agency.
MS	Registered sex offenders may not be present on school property.	Fingerprint-based FBI and state criminal history checks are required of all public school employees and substitute teachers.	Public schools may not employ individuals convicted of a violent or sexual felony or of child abuse.	Superintendents must notify law enforcement of all crimes that occur on school property. Public and private school employees who have reasonable cause to suspect a child is abused or neglected must notify the Depart-ment of Human Services.

Appendix I. (Continued)

State	Prohibitions on sex offenders working in or being present at schools	Criminal history check requirements for school employees, contractors, and volunteers	Offenses requiring mandatory termination of employment or revocation of license	Mandatory reporting requirements
MO	Registered sex offenders whose victims were minors may not be present on school property or at a school activity without permission and may not serve as a coach or manager for any youth sports team.	Fingerprint-based FBI and state criminal history checks are required of all certified teachers and public school employees and bus drivers.	None located.	Principals must report all sexual assaults to law enforcement. School teachers and officials who have reasonable cause to suspect that a child has been subjected to abuse or neglect must notify the Department of Social Services.
MT	A mandatory condition of probation/parole for sexual offenders is employment restrictions to protect potential future victims of the offender.	None located.	None located.	School districts must report the dismissal or resignation of teachers and administrators resulting from a felony conviction or immoral conduct to the state Super-intendent of Public Instruction. School employees who have reasonable cause to suspect child abuse or neglect must notify the Department of Public Health and Human Services.
NE	None located.	Fingerprint-based FBI and state criminal history checks required of all certified teachers and administrators if they have not been state residents for previous 5 years.	None located.	School employees who have reasonable cause to suspect a child has been subject to abuse or neglect must notify law enforcement or the NE Department of Health & Human Services.

State	Prohibitions on sex offenders working in or being present at schools	Criminal history check requirements for school employees, contractors, and volunteers	Offenses requiring mandatory termination of employment or revocation of license	Mandatory reporting requirements
NV	A mandatory condition of probation/parole for sexual offenders is a prohibition on coming within 500 feet of a school.	Fingerprint-based FBI and state criminal history checks are required of all licensed teachers and public and charter school employees.	Convicted felons or offenders with convictions involving moral turpitude are ineligible for a teaching license.	Teachers who know or have reasonable cause to believe that a child has been abused or neglected must notify law enforcement or a child welfare agency.
NH	None located.	Fingerprint-based FBI and state criminal history checks are required of all public and charter school employees, volunteers, and contractor employees. Private schools are authorized to conduct such checks of their employees. Criminal history checks are required of all applicants for a school bus license.	Public schools may not employ felons convicted of murder, sexual assault, child pornography, or kidnapping.	School teachers and officials who suspect child abuse or neglect must notify the NH Department of Health & Human Services.
NJ	None located.	Fingerprint-based FBI and state criminal history checks are required of all public school employees and selected contractor employees (including school bus drivers). Public schools are also authorized to conduct such	Public schools may not employ or use as contractor employees persons convicted of a felony in the first or second degree.	Any person with reasonable cause to believe that a child has been subjected to child abuse must notify the Division of Youth and Family Services.

Appendix I. (Continued)

State	Prohibitions on sex offenders working in or being present at schools	Criminal history check requirements for school employees, contractors, and volunteers	Offenses requiring mandatory termination of employment or revocation of license	Mandatory reporting requirements
		checks on volunteers with regular contact with children. Private schools are authorized to conduct such background checks of their employees and contractor employees.		
NM	None located.	Fingerprint-based FBI criminal history checks are required of all licensed teachers and public school employees and contractor employees.	None located.	Superintendents must notify the NM Department of Education when a licensed educator is dismissed or resigns resulting from allegations of misconduct. School teachers and officials who know or reason-ably suspect child abuse or neglect must notify law enforcement or the Children, Youth & Families Department.
NY	A mandatory condition of parole for sexual offenders whose victims were minors is a prohibition on entering school grounds.	Fingerprint-based FBI and state criminal history checks and background checks are required of all certified teachers and public school employees. Private schools are authorized to conduct such background checks of their employees and volunteers.	Public schools may not employ registered sex offenders. Felons convicted of certain violent or sexual offenses may not hold a school bus driver license.	School administerators or superintend dents must notify law enforcement of allegations of child abuse in an educational setting. School personnel with reasonable cause to suspect child abuse must notify the Office of Children & Family Services.

State	Prohibitions on sex offenders working in or being present at schools	Criminal history check requirements for school employees, contractors, and volunteers	Offenses requiring mandatory termination of employment or revocation of license	Mandatory reporting requirements
NC	Registered sex offenders may not be present on school property or work or volunteer at any position involving the supervision, care, or instruction of minors.	Public school districts are required to have a policy determining which employees and contract employees are subject to fingerprint-based FBI and state criminal history checks.	None located.	Principals must report any sexual offenses occurring on school property to law enforcement, and school boards must notify the parents of such victims. Anyone who has cause to suspect child abuse or neglect must notify the Department of Social Services.
ND	Registered sex offenders whose victims were minors may not be present on school property.	Fingerprint-based national and state criminal history checks are required of all licensed teachers, school counselors, and public and private school employees with unsupervised contact with children.	None located.	School teachers and administrators with reasonable cause to suspect that a child is abused or neglected must notify the Department of Human Services.

Appendix I. (Continued)

State	Prohibitions on sex offenders working in or being present at schools	Criminal history check requirements for school employees, contractors, and volunteers	Offenses requiring mandatory termination of employment or revocation of license	Mandatory reporting requirements
OH	None located.	Fingerprint-based FBI and state criminal history checks are required of all licensed educators, preschool employees, public school contractor employees with unsupervised access to children, and school bus license holders. Such checks are required of all public or charter school employees every 5 years; however, the FBI check is not required if the employee has been a resident of Ohio for the past 5 years.	Public and charter schools, school bus operators, and preschools may not employ a person convicted of a violent or sexual offense. Conviction of a felony is grounds for revocation of an educator licensing.	School teachers and employees who have reasonable cause to suspect child abuse or neglect must notify law enforcement or a public children services agency.
OK	Registered sex offenders may not work on school premises or loiter within 500 feet of a school.	Fingerprint-based national and state criminal history checks are required of all licensed teachers. Public school districts are required to implement a criminal history check policy for all employees.	None located.	Any person who has reason to believe a child is a victim of abuse or neglect must notify the state hotline.

State	Prohibitions on sex offenders working in or being present at schools	Criminal history check requirements for school employees, contractors, and volunteers	Offenses requiring mandatory termination of employment or revocation of license	Mandatory reporting requirements
OR	Predatory and violent sex offenders may not be on school premises.	Fingerprint-based national and state criminal history checks are required of all licensed teachers. Public schools are required to conduct such checks of their employees and contractors. Private schools are authorized to conduct such checks.	Felons convicted of certain violent or sexual offenses may not hold a teaching license.	School employees who have reason-able cause to suspect child abuse must notify law enforcement or the Department of Human Services. School boards must adopt policies requiring employees to report such abuse.
		Public and private schools are authorized to conduct state criminal checks on their volunteers with direct, unsupervised contact with children.		
PA	None located.	State criminal history checks are required of all public and private school employees and contractor employees who have direct contact with children. If the individual has not been a state resident for at least 2 years prior, then a fingerprint -based FBI criminal history check is required. Public schools are required to conduct an abuse registry check on all new employees.	Public and private schools may not employ felons convicted of certain violent or sexual offenses within the past 5 years or persons listed as a perpetrator of child abuse.	Superintendents must report information which constitutes reason-able cause to believe that a licensed educator has committed sexual abuse to the PA Department of Education. School administrators and teachers who have reasonable cause to suspect child abuse must notify the Department of Public Welfare.

Appendix I. (Continued)

State	Prohibitions on sex offenders working in or being present at schools	Criminal history check requirements for school employees, contractors, and volunteers	Offenses requiring mandatory termination of employment or revocation of license	Mandatory reporting requirements
RI	None located.	Fingerprint-based national and state criminal history checks are required of all public and private school employees.	None located.	Any person who has reasonable cause to suspect child abuse must notify the Department of Children, Youth & Families.
SC	None located.	State name-based criminal history checks and national sex offender registry checks are required of all public school employees, volunteers, and school bus drivers.	Public schools may not hire anyone convicted of a violelnt crime.	Any crimes committed in a school must be reported to law enforcement. Teachers and principals who have reason to believe a child has been abused or neglected must notify law enforcement.
SD	Registered sex offenders may not loiter within 500 feet of a school.	Fingerprint-based national and state criminal history checks are required of all public school employees.	Public schools may not hire or contract with felons convicted of violent, drug, or sexual offenses.	Public and private school teachers and officials who have reasonable cause to suspect child abuse or neglect must notify their principal or superintendent who must notify law enforcement, a state's attorney, or the Department of Social Services.
TN	Registered sex offenders whose victims were minors may not be employed within 1000 feet of school property.	Fingerprint-based national and state criminal history checks are required of all public school teachers and employees or contractual employees in positions requiring proximity to children. Criminal history checks are required of all school bus license holders.	Felons convicted of certain violent or sexual offenses may not hold a teaching license. Sexual offenders may not come into direct contact with children.	School personnel who have reason-able cause to suspect child abuse must report it to a juvenile judge, law enforcement, or the Department of Children's Services. If the abuse occurred on school grounds, then the parents of the victim must also be given notice.

State	Prohibitions on sex offenders working in or being present at schools	Criminal history check requirements for school employees, contractors, and volunteers	Offenses requiring mandatory termination of employment or revocation of license	Mandatory reporting requirements
TX	A mandatory condition of parole for sexual offenders whose victims were minors is a prohibition on entering school property.	National criminal history checks are required of all certified educators, public school employees and contractor employees (with direct contact with students), student teachers, volunteers, substitute teachers, and bus drivers. Private schools are authorized to conduct such checks of their employees, volunteers, and contractor employees.	Public schools may not hire persons or use contractor employees with felony or sex offender convictions. Bus driver operators may not employ individuals with felony or misdemeanor (involving moral turpitude) convictions.	Superintendents must notify the State Board for Educator Certification if an educator is terminated for abusing a student. Principals must notify law enforcement when a felony is committed on school property. Teachers who have cause to believe that a child's physical or mental health or welfare has been adversely affected by abuse or neglect must notify a state agency or law enforcement.
UT	Registered sex offenders may not enter school premises.	Fingerprint-based criminal history checks are required of all public school employees and volunteers and employees and volunteers of private schools that accept state scholarships. Other private schools are authorized to conduct criminal history checks of their employees.	None located.	Any person who has reason to believe that a child has been subjected to abuse or neglect must notify law enforcement or the Division of Child and Family Services.
VT	None located.	Fingerprint-based FBI and state criminal background and abuse registry checks are required of all licensed educators and public and independent school employees and contractor employees.	Sex offenders are ineligible for public or independent school employment.	Any person who has reasonable cause to believe that a licensed educator has engaged in unprofessional conduct must notify the VT Department of Education. School district employees, teachers, or principals who have reasonable cause to believe that any child has been abused or neglected must notify the Department for Children & Families.

Appendix I. (Continued)

State	Prohibitions on sex offenders working in or being present at schools	Criminal history check requirements for school employees, contractors, and volunteers	Offenses requiring mandatory termination of employment or revocation of license	Mandatory reporting requirements
VA	Sexually violent offenders may not enter school property.	Fingerprint-based national and state criminal history checks are required of all public school employees and accredited private school employees.	Persons convicted of sexual molestation, sexual abuse, rape a child are ineligible or public school employment or with a contractor who provides services to public schools. Persons found to be perpetrator of child abuse ineligible for public school employment.	School boards must notify the Board of Education when licensed educators are dismissed or resign as a result of a sexual offense. Public and private school employees who have reason to suspect child abuse or neglect must notify the local child-protective services unit or a state hotline.
WA	A mandatory condition of supervised release for sexual offenders whose victims were minors prohibition on serving in a paid or volunteer capacity in a position involving control supervision of children.	Fingerprint-based national and state criminal history checks are required of all public school employees, volunteers, and contractor employees.	Conviction of a felony against a child is grounds for permanent revocation of a teaching certificate.	Public school employees who have reasonable cause to believe that a student is the victim of sexual misconduct by a school employee must notify the school's administrator, who must notify law enforcement. Professional school personnel who have reason-able cause to believe that a child has suffered abuse or neglect must notify law enforcement or the Department of Social & Health Services.
WV	A mandatory condition of supervised release for sexual offenders whose victims were minors is a prohibition on employment within 1000 feet of a school.	Fingerprint-based FBI and state criminal history checks are required of all licensed teachers. School bus drivers are also subject to criminal history checks.	None located.	School teachers and personnel who have reasonable cause to suspect sexual abuse of a child must notify law enforcement and the Department of Health and Human Resources.

State	Prohibitions on sex offenders working in or being present at schools	Criminal history check requirements for school employees, contractors, and volunteers	Offenses requiring mandatory termination of employment or revocation of license	Mandatory reporting requirements
WI	Convicted sex offenders whose victims were minors may not be employed or volunteer in a position that requires interaction with children.	State criminal history checks are required of all licensed teachers. Fingerprint-based FBI criminal history checks are required of all teacher license applicants who have not been state residents. A state criminal history check is required of all school bus license applicants, and a federal background check is required if the applicant had not resided in the state at any time during the preceding 2 years.	Individuals convicted of violent or child-victim crimes during the past 6 years are ineligible for a teacher license. Individuals convicted of violent or sexual or child-victim crimes during the past 5 years are ineligible for a school bus license.	School administrators must report to the State Super-intendent if a licensed educator is charged with a sexual offense or is dismissed or resigns as a result of immoral conduct. School teachers and administrators who have reason-able cause to suspect that a child has been abused or neglected must notify law enforcement or the local child welfare agency.
WY	Registered sex offenders may not be present on school grounds.	Fingerprint-based national and state criminal history checks are required of all certified teachers and public school employees with access to minors.	None located.	School boards must notify the state teaching board if a licensed educator is dismissed or resigns as a result of a felony conviction. Any person who has reasonable cause to believe or suspect that a child has been abused or neglected must notify the child protective agency or law enforcement.

Source: GAO analysis of relevant state laws.

End Notes

[1] GAO, *Residential Treatment Programs: Concerns Regarding Abuse and Death in Certain Programs for Troubled Youth*, GAO-08-146T (Washington, D.C.: Oct. 10, 2007); *Residential Programs: Selected Cases of Death, Abuse, and Deceptive Marketing*, GAO-08-713T (Washington, D.C.: Apr. 24, 2008); and *Seclusions and Restraints: Selected Cases of Death and Abuse at Public and Private Schools and Treatment Centers*, GAO-09-719T (Washington, D.C.: May 19, 2009).

[2] The center was established in 1984 as a private, nonprofit organization to provide services nationwide for families and professionals in the prevention of abducted, endangered, and sexually exploited children. The center receives funding from the Office of Juvenile Justice and Delinquency Prevention, a component of the Department of Justice's Office of Justice Programs.

[3] GAO, *Convicted Sex Offenders: Factors That Could Affect the Successful Implementation of Driver's License-Related Processes to Encourage Registration and Enhance Monitoring*, GAO-08-116 (Washington, D.C.: January 2008)

[4] These states and the District of Columbia are not a sample, but illustrate a broad range of size and location.

[5] For this work, we used the sensitive, nonpublic NSOR. The public national sex offender registry, as accessed through the Dru Sjodin National Sex Offender Public Web site, does not contain offender SSNs, and does not disclose information on all registered sex offenders. Some states use a tiered ranking system for evaluating the potential danger posed by individual sex offenders. For these states, the information on some of the low-risk tiers of sex offenders may be withheld from public disclosure. However, these nonpublic sex offenders are still subject to all sex offender registration requirements, such as requirements to disclose changes in address and employment, and to provide current photographs to law enforcement.

[6] Schools were identified using keyword searches for employers whose business names contained terms such as "school," "academy," or "education."

[7] Although the school principal denied providing this reference, she told us that a staff member may have done so in her absence.

[8] Employees provide fingerprints at the time of hire and schools are later notified by California law enforcement authorities if an individual providing a matching fingerprint is arrested.

[9] The current superintendent of the school system was not in office when the investigation occurred.

[10] Though the teacher submitted a letter of resignation, he did protest the investigation, arguing that other teachers at the school were maliciously targeting him.

[11] He had previously been convicted in California in 1979 of battery.

[12] According to the superintendent of this school district, as a result of this incident, since fall 2009 the district hiring procedures for teachers now include an additional reference check directly with the human resources department of all prior places of employment concerning the circumstances of an applicant's separation from employment. The superintendent told us that sometimes the terms of a "letter of separation" can prevent a principal from disclosing information which a representative from human resources could disclose.

[13] The teacher's certificate was revoked in November 2009 after his criminal conviction.

[14] Arizona law requires criminal history checks for all public school employees.

[15] Since the time of this case study, the school district has purchased an electronic fingerprint machine which returns the results of a fingerprint check immediately.

[16] Arkansas, Delaware, Idaho, Illinois, Kentucky, Louisiana, Maryland, Michigan, Mississippi, Missouri, North Carolina, North Dakota, Oklahoma, Oregon, South Dakota, Utah, Virginia, and Wyoming.

[17] Alabama, California, Florida, Georgia, Illinois, Indiana, Iowa, Louisiana, Michigan, Missouri, Montana, North Carolina, Oklahoma, Tennessee, Washington, West Virginia, and Wisconsin.

[18] Kansas and Montana.

[19] Arizona, Arkansas, Colorado, Connecticut, Delaware, Georgia, Kentucky, Louisiana, Maine, Minnesota, Mississippi, Missouri, Nevada, New Hampshire, New Jersey, New Mexico, New York, Ohio, Oklahoma, Oregon, South Carolina, South Dakota, Tennessee, Texas, and Washington.

[20] Florida, Illinois, Indiana, Massachusetts, Utah, and Virginia.

[21] Alabama, California, Maryland, Michigan, Pennsylvania, Rhode Island, and Vermont.

[22] Alaska, Iowa, West Virginia, and Wisconsin.

[23] Hawaii, Idaho, North Dakota, and Wyoming.

[24] Nebraska.

[25] North Carolina.

[26] California, Indiana, Massachusetts, Michigan, and Vermont. Pennsylvania requires such checks if the contractors have direct contact with children.

[27] Arizona, Illinois, New Hampshire, New Mexico, North Carolina, Oregon, and Washington.

[28] Arizona, Massachusetts, Minnesota, New Hampshire, New Jersey, South Carolina, Texas, Utah, and Washington.

[29] Minnesota and South Carolina.

[30] Pennsylvania.

[31] E.g., Massachusetts, Ohio, and Florida.

[32] E.g., Michigan and California.

[33] E.g., Minnesota.

[34] E.g., Louisiana.

[35] E.g., Nevada.

In: K-12 Education Challenges
Editors: A.Hernandez and S. Jordan

ISBN 978-1-61942-870-6
© 2012 Nova Science Publishers, Inc.

Chapter 2

K-12 EDUCATION: MANY CHALLENGES ARISE IN EDUCATING STUDENTS WHO CHANGE SCHOOLS FREQUENTLY[*]

United States Government Accountability Office

WHY GAO DID THIS STUDY

Educational achievement of students can be negatively affected by their changing schools often. The recent economic downturn, with foreclosures and homelessness, may be increasing student mobility.

To inform Elementary and Secondary Education Act of 1965 (ESEA) reauthorization, GAO was asked: (1) What are the numbers and characteristics of students who change schools, and what are the reasons students change schools? (2)What is known about the effects of mobility on student outcomes, including academic achievement, behavior, and other outcomes? (3) What challenges does student mobility present for schools in meeting the educational needs of students who change schools? (4) What key federal programs are schools using to address the needs of mobile students? GAO analyzed federal survey data, interviewed U.S. Department of Education (Education) officials, conducted site visits at eight schools in six school districts, and reviewed federal laws and existing research.

---

[*] This is an edited, reformatted and augmented version of Highlights of GAO-11-40, a report to congressional requesters, dated November 2010.

WHAT GAO RECOMMENDS

GAO is not making recommendations in this report. Education had no comments on this report.

WHAT GAO FOUND

While nearly all students change schools at some point before reaching high school, some change schools with greater frequency. According to Education's national survey data, the students who change schools the most frequently (four or more times) represented about 13 percent of all kindergarten through eighth grade (K-8) students and they were disproportionately poor, African American, and from families that did not own their home. About 11.5 percent of schools also had high rates of mobility— more than 10 percent of K-8 students left by the end of the school year. These schools, in addition to serving a mobile population, had larger percentages of students who were low-income, received special education, and had limited English proficiency.

Research suggests that mobility is one of several interrelated factors, such as socio-economic status and lack of parental education, which have a negative effect on academic achievement, but research about mobility's effect on students' social and emotional well-being is limited and inconclusive. With respect to academic achievement, students who change schools more frequently tend to have lower scores on standardized reading and math tests and drop out of school at higher rates than their less mobile peers.

Schools face a range of challenges in meeting the academic, social, and emotional needs of students who change schools. Teachers we interviewed said that students who change schools often face challenges due to differences in what is taught and how it is taught. Students may arrive without records or with incomplete records, making it difficult for teachers to make placement decisions and identify special education needs. Also, teachers and principals told us that schools face challenges in supporting the needs of these students' families, the circumstances of which often underlie frequent school changes. Moreover, these schools face the dual challenge of educating a mobile student population, as well as a general student population, that is often largely low-income and disadvantaged.

Schools use a range of federal programs already in place and targeted to at- risk students to meet the needs of students who change schools frequently. Teachers and principals told us that mobile students are often eligible for and benefit from federal programs for low-income, disadvantaged students, such as Title 1, Part A of ESEA which funds tutoring and after-school instruction. In addition, school officials we interviewed said they rely on the McKinney-Vento Education for Homeless Children and Youth Program, which provides such things as clothing and school supplies to homeless students and requires schools to provide transportation for homeless students who lack permanent residence so they can avoid changing schools. GAO did not evaluate the effectiveness of these programs in meeting the needs of mobile students.

ABBREVIATIONS

ECLS-K	Early Childhood Longitudinal Study: Kindergarten Class of 1998-1999
ESEA	Elementary and Secondary Education Act of 1965
IDEA	Individuals with Disabilities Education Act
NAEP	National Assessment of Educational Progress
NCES	National Center for Education Statistics
NSLP	National School Lunch Program
NCLB	No Child Left Behind Act of 2001
Recovery Act	American Recovery and Reinvestment Act of 2009
TANF	Temporary Assistance for Needy Families Program

November 18, 2010

The Honorable Tom Harkin
Chairman
Committee on Health, Education, Labor, and Pensions
United States Senate

The Honorable Christopher J. Dodd
Chairman
Subcommittee on Children and Families
Committee on Health, Education, Labor, and Pensions
United States Senate

56 United States Government Accountability Office

Although the landmark Elementary and Secondary Education Act of 1965 (ESEA) was enacted more than 40 years ago to help improve the educational outcomes of our nation's poor children, the achievement gap continues to persist and grow between them and their more affluent peers. Research suggests that poor students change schools more frequently than other students and that these school changes can disrupt their education. Moreover, the recent economic downturn, which resulted in job loss, foreclosures, and homelessness for many Americans, may be increasing the numbers and frequency of students changing schools as their families relocate in search of employment and affordable housing.

In preparation for the reauthorization of ESEA, the Chairman of the Senate Committee on Health, Education, Labor, and Pensions, and the Chairman of its Subcommittee on Children and Families asked GAO to undertake a study of the scope of student mobility in the United States today and examine its effect on students and schools. Specifically, we were asked to address the following questions: (1) What are the numbers and characteristics of students who change schools, and what are the reasons students change schools? (2) What is known about the effects of mobility on student outcomes, including academic achievement, behavior, and other outcomes? (3) What challenges does student mobility present for schools in meeting the educational needs of students who change schools? (4) What key federal programs are schools using to address the needs of mobile students?

To answer these questions, we analyzed two nationally representative datasets from the Department of Education (Education): one, which followed a cohort of students from 1998 to 2007, contained information on the numbers and characteristics of mobile students and the other contained information on the schools students attended in 2007.[1] Neither of these datasets allowed us to assess effects of the economic downturn on student mobility, which occurred post 2007. To collect additional information about the mobile student population and reasons for their mobility, including any potential effects of the recent economic downturn, we interviewed school officials and federal and state education officials. We determined that Education's data were sufficiently reliable and valid for the purposes of our review. We reviewed external studies that measured the effects of student mobility on both educational and noneducational student outcomes. We selected studies that were published during or after 1984 and contained original data analysis or meta-analysis. We conducted site visits to a nonprobability sample of eight schools across six school districts in three states (California, Michigan, and Texas) where we interviewed school officials and parents about the challenges of student mobility and how schools address those challenges. We selected states that provided geographic coverage and that had high percentages of economically disadvantaged students and/or high rates of foreclosures to provide insight on how the economic downturn might be affecting students and schools in high poverty areas. We selected schools with high percentages of mobile students and that differed by school type (public and charter), grade level (elementary, middle, and high school), and location (urban, suburban, and rural). We interviewed federal, state, and school officials about federal programs that serve low-income, disadvantaged, and special needs students, including those who change schools, and we reviewed relevant federal laws, regulations, and agency documents. In addition, we interviewed state education officials and local homeless education liaisons about federal efforts to assist mobile students from homeless families.[2] (See appendix I for a detailed description of this study's scope and methodology.)

We conducted this performance audit from October 2009 through November 2010 in accordance with generally accepted government auditing standards. Those standards require that we plan and perform the audit to obtain sufficient, appropriate evidence to provide a reasonable basis for our findings and conclusions based on our audit objectives. We believe that the evidence obtained provides a reasonable basis for our findings and conclusions based on our audit objectives.

BACKGROUND

Nearly all students change school at some point during their school years, most typically when they are promoted to a higher grade at a different school. Specifically, students may change schools as they are promoted from elementary to middle school and again from middle to high school. In addition, students may also change schools when their families move to a new home or to relocate closer to jobs.

In 1994, we issued a report that highlighted concerns about the education of elementary school students who changed schools more frequently than the norm.[3] This report found that one in six third graders changed schools frequently, attending at least three different schools since the beginning of first grade. Students who changed schools frequently were often from low- income families, the inner city, migrant families, or had limited English proficiency. These highly mobile students had low math and reading scores and were more likely to repeat a grade. We recommended that Education ensure low-income

58 United States Government Accountability Office

students have access to ESEA's Title I services,[4] which they have taken steps to do so.

Since we issued our 1994 report, policymakers have continued to focus attention on students' educational achievement. Specifically, the No Child Left Behind Act of 2001 (NCLBA), which reauthorized ESEA, established a deadline of 2014 for all students to reach proficiency in reading, math, and science. Under NCLBA, districts and schools must demonstrate adequate yearly progress toward meeting state standards for all students and every key subgroup of students, including low-income students, minority students, students with disabilities, and students with limited English proficiency.

CHARACTERISTICS OF MORE MOBILE AND LESS MOBILE STUDENTS AND THEIR SCHOOLS DIFFER

While nearly all students change schools at some point before reaching high school, some students change schools with greater frequency (see figure 1). According to Education data, which followed a cohort of kindergarteners from 1998 to 2007, the majority of students—about 70 percent—changed schools two times or less and about 18 percent changed three times before reaching high school.[5] Some of these school changes could occur as a result of students being promoted to a higher grade in a different school or parents moving to a new home or relocating closer to their jobs.

However, for the students who changed schools four or more times (about 13 percent), our analysis of Education's data revealed statistically significant differences between them and students who had changed two times or less, not only in the frequency of their changes but along several important dimensions. We compared students who changed schools two or fewer times (referred to in this report as "less mobile") to students who changed schools four or more times (referred to as "more mobile"). We selected this comparison because the differences were most pronounced and because the two groups combined represent a significant fraction (about 82 percent) of the population of the students in the cohort. We also found statistically significant differences between students who changed schools two or fewer times and students who changed schools three or more times, but these differences were less pronounced. See appendix II for Education's *Early Childhood Longitudinal Study: Kindergarten Class of 1998-1999* (ECLS-K) data on the mobile student population.

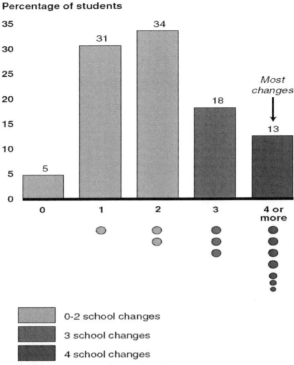

Source: GAO analysis of ECLS-K data, 1998-2007.
Note: Percentages do not add to 100 due to rounding.

Figure 1. Number of Times Students Changed Schools Between Kindergarten and Eighth Grades.

Students who changed schools four or more times were disproportionately poor, African American, and from families that did not own their home or have a father present in the household. These more mobile students— compared to those who changed schools two times or less—had a significantly larger percentage of students with family incomes below the poverty threshold, according to Education's survey data.[6] Furthermore, a significantly larger percentage of the more mobile students, compared to less mobile students, received benefits under the National School Lunch Program (NSLP), the Supplemental Nutrition Assistance Program, and the Temporary Assistance for Needy Families (TANF) program.[7] As shown in figure 2, about 26 percent of students who changed schools four or more times had family incomes below the poverty threshold, compared to about 17 percent of the students who changed schools two times or less. Moreover, significantly smaller percentages of the more mobile students had a father present in the household, when compared to their less mobile peers who changed schools two times or less.

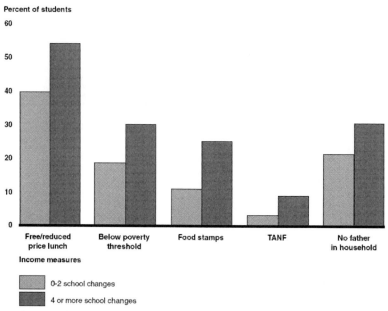

Source: GAO analysis of ECLS-K data, 1998-2007.

Notes: Estimates in this figure compare the percentage of all students who changed schools two times or less that had these characteristics to the percentage of all students who changed schools four or more times who also had these characteristics. For example, as depicted in the graph, 40 percent of all students who changed two times or less and 54 percent of all students who changed four or more times received free or reduced price lunch.

Except where otherwise noted, all results for all figures presenting student data were statistically significant at the 95 percent confidence level.

Figure 2. Comparison Across Income Measures for Less Mobile and More Mobile Students.

African-American students comprised a disproportionately larger percentage of the students who changed schools four or more times when compared to African-American students, as well as all other racial ethnic groups, who changed schools two times or less, as shown in figure 3.[8] African-American students represented about 15 percent of students in kindergarten through eighth grade who changed schools two times or less; however, they represented about 23 percent of students who changed schools four or more times. In contrast, white students, who represented about 60 percent of all students in the same grade range who changed schools two times or less, accounted for about 51 percent of students who changed schools four times or more.

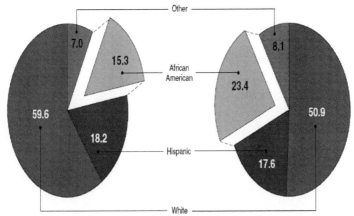

Source: GAO analysis of ECLS-K data, 1998-2007.

Figure 3. Comparison Across Race for Less Mobile and More Mobile Students.

Finally, a significantly larger percentage of students who changed schools four or more times came from families that did not own their home. Students from families that did not own their own home represented about 39 percent of students who changed schools four or more times compared to about 20 percent for those who changed schools two or fewer times—a difference of about 100 percent. According to principals and teachers we interviewed, the more mobile students' families may rent, live with relatives, or move back and forth between relatives and friends. Further, some students may be homeless; however, teachers and other school officials we interviewed said that, in some cases, it may be difficult to know whether a student is homeless because families may not disclose that they are homeless or may not consider their particular living arrangements as being homeless, for example, staying with relatives or doubling up—that is, living with another family or families in a residence designed for a single family.[9] See appendix II for additional information about the mobile student population.

The schools with the highest rates of student mobility also showed differences across several characteristics. According to Education's data, about

11.5 percent of schools had the highest rates of student mobility— those where more than 10 percent of their eighth grade students started the year at the school but left by the end of the school year.[10] These schools had larger percentages of at-risk eighth grade students compared to schools where less than 10 percent of the students changed schools. According to Education's data, these schools had larger percentages of eighth grade students eligible for Title I assistance, the federal government's largest program for low-income school age children. For example, about 62 percent of the schools with high mobility rates received Title I funding, compared to about 46 percent of the schools where students' mobility rates were lower. Moreover, the schools with high mobility rates were more often eligible for Title I "school-wide" programs, a designation that allows schools with a population of at least 40 percent low-income students, to offer services to every student in the school. As shown in figure 4, about 45 percent of the schools with high mobility rates were classified as school-wide, compared to about 21 percent of the schools that had lower rates of student mobility.

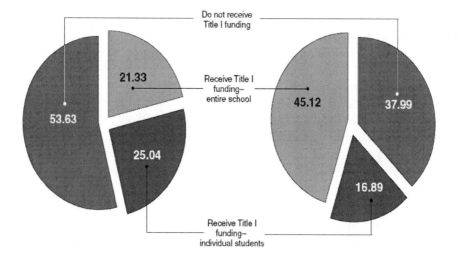

Source: GAO analysis of NAEP data, 2007.
Note: Except otherwise noted, all results for all figures presenting school data were statistically significant at the 95 percent confidence level.

Figure 4. Comparison of Schools with Low and High Mobility Rates Receiving School-wide Title I Funding.

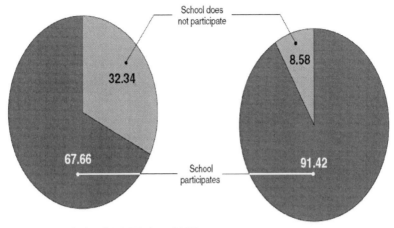

Source: GAO analysis of NAEP data, 2007.

Figure 5. Comparison of Schools with Low and High Mobility Rates That Participate in NSLP.

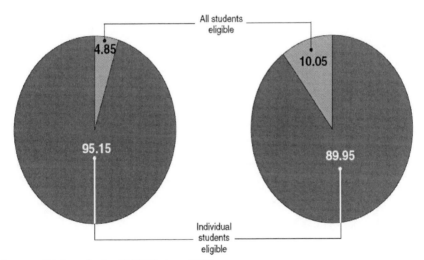

Source: GAO analysis of NAEP data, 2007.

Figure 6. Comparison of Schools with Low and High Mobility Rates Regarding Student Eligibility for NSLP.

Moreover, the schools with high mobility rates were more likely to participate in NSLP. Specifically, as shown in figure 5, about 91 percent of the schools with high mobility rates participated in the school lunch program, compared to about 68 percent of the schools with lower rates of student mobility.

In addition, for about 10 percent of the schools with high mobility rates, all of the students in these schools were eligible for free or reduced-price lunch, compared to about 5 percent of the schools with lower rates of student mobility (see figure 6).

The schools with high mobility rates also had larger percentages of eighth grade students receiving special education services, with limited English proficiency, and having higher rates of absenteeism. Specifically, as shown in figure 7, of the schools that had 11-25 percent of their eighth grade students receiving special education services, about 50 percent had high mobility rates compared to about 32 percent that had lower rates of mobility.

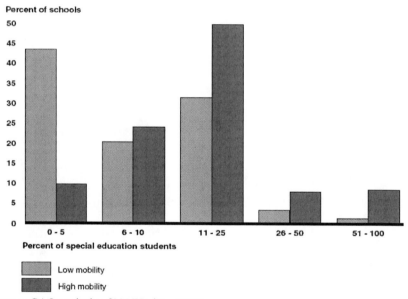

Source: GAO analysis of NAEP data, 2007.

Figure 7. Comparison of Schools with Low and High Mobility Rates Regarding Special Education Students.

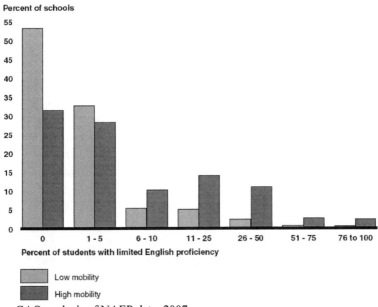

Source: GAO analysis of NAEP data, 2007.

Figure 8. Comparison of Schools with Low and High Mobility Rates Regarding Students Who Have Limited English Proficiency.

Schools with high mobility rates also had larger percentages of their eighth grade students who had limited English proficiency. For example, as shown in figure 8, of the schools that had 26-50 percent of students with limited English proficiency, about 11 percent had high mobility rates compared to about 2 percent that had lower rates of mobility.

Finally, the schools with high mobility rates had larger percentages of students absent. About 30 percent of the schools with high mobility rates had 6-10 percent of students absent on an average day, compared to about 11 percent of the schools with lower rates of mobility. See appendix III for additional information comparing schools with high rates of mobility to schools with less mobility.

Teachers, principals, and parents told us that financial difficulties and family instability often underlie why students change schools frequently, but some cited other reasons as well, such as parents' desire to send their children to a better-performing or safer school. Some school officials and parents in all three states we visited (California, Michigan, and Texas) said that economic difficulties, including job loss, played a role in student mobility. For example, the principal of one Detroit-area school serving a large low-income population said that families lost their jobs when the automobile industry declined and moved out of the area in search of jobs. Several principals and teachers also cited foreclosures on homes and the inability of some families to pay the rent as reasons that students changed schools. For example, officials at a rural California high school said that relatively inexpensive real estate attracted many homeowners who later lost their homes. One teacher in California told us that some families who are unable to pay the rent and are evicted will move from one apartment complex to another complex offering a free month's rent. In addition, school officials in all three states we visited said that they saw more families "doubled-up"—sharing a single-family residence with one or more other families. School officials said all of these situations have resulted in students changing schools.

Family instability also plays a role in mobility, according to parents and school officials we interviewed. School officials in all three states we visited cited divorce as a reason for mobility. For example, school officials in Michigan told us that one student had changed schools four times during one school year when his parents' custody arrangement changed. In an urban school in Texas and a rural school in California, teachers and principals also said that school changes can result when students are passed around among relatives or friends when there is conflict in the student's family. Officials in California and Michigan told us that mobility also results when social services personnel need to remove students from their homes and that foster children are highly mobile, too. In addition to family issues, school officials and parents in all three states said that, in some cases, mobility results from family choice related to safety concerns or the desire to provide different educational options for their children. For example, one parent in Texas said she changed residences and her child's school after two home break-ins and in California, a principal said that some families come to his school district to escape gang activity and violence.

RESEARCH SUGGESTS STUDENT MOBILITY CAN HAVE A NEGATIVE EFFECT ON ACADEMIC ACHIEVEMENT, BUT ITS EFFECT ON SOCIAL ADJUSTMENT IS UNCLEAR

A body of research suggests that student mobility has a negative effect on students' academic achievement, but research on its effect on their social and emotional well-being is inconclusive. With respect to academic outcomes, while research suggests that the academic achievement of students is affected by a set of interrelated factors that includes socioeconomic status and parental education, there is evidence that mobility has an effect on achievement apart from these other factors.[11] Specifically, the body of research suggests that students who changed schools more frequently tended to have lower scores on standardized reading and math tests and to drop out of school at higher rates than their less mobile peers.[12] For example, a national study that tracked high school age students found that changing high schools was associated with lower performance on math and reading tests. Another study using the same national, longitudinal dataset found that students who changed schools two or more times from 8th to 12th grade were twice as likely to drop out of high school, or not obtain a General Equivalency Diploma, compared to students who did not change schools. In addition, a meta-analysis found that student mobility was associated with lower achievement and higher rates of high school dropout.[13]

Further, some studies found that the effect of mobility on achievement varied depending on other factors, such as the student's race/ethnicity, special needs, grade level, frequency of school change, and characteristics of the school change—whether it was between school districts or within a district, or whether it was to an urban or suburban/rural district.[14] For example, one study found that school changes from one school district to another tended to result in long-term changes in academic performance and that this long-term change tended to be positive for students who moved to schools in nonurban districts[15] but negative for those who moved to urban areas. In addition, this study found that school changes within the same school district were not associated with any long-term changes in performance, but were associated with short-run negative effects on performance that were generally greater for African-American, Hispanic, and poor students.

The small body of research that exists about the effect of mobility on students' social and emotional well-being is limited and inconclusive. These studies generally used methods that do not support strong conclusions about specific relationships between mobility and social and behavioral outcomes. One important limitation is that these studies typically did not account for pre-existing differences between more mobile and less mobile students. For example, we were unable to report the results of two national longitudinal studies that we reviewed because the studies used narrow, limited measures of student behavior and other social outcomes, and the studies did not control for prior student behavior and social conditions. A complete list of the studies we reviewed is included in appendix IV.

SCHOOLS WITH HIGH STUDENT MOBILITY FACE CHALLENGES IN MEETING THE ACADEMIC AND EMOTIONAL NEEDS OF ALL STUDENTS

Officials we interviewed in schools with high rates of student mobility said they often face the dual challenge of meeting the needs of their students who change schools at high rates and the needs of the entire student body, which is comprised largely of low-income, disadvantaged students. A number of teachers and principals told us that when new students arrive, it can sometimes affect the pace of instruction for the entire classroom, as teachers attend to the needs of a new student. Moreover, some teachers and principals said that for a new student, there may be differences in what and how instruction has been delivered to them from school to school, and this can make it difficult for teachers to assess where students are academically when they arrive and make decisions about proper placement. Further, teachers in two schools said that the order in which course material is taught varies from school to school, presenting challenges for teachers in the classrooms. For example, one teacher told about a student who moved to Texas from California and was placed in an algebra class based on her academic record, but was later moved to a more appropriate class after the teachers saw her struggling to keep up with her peers. Also, a teacher from a Texas middle school, whose district teaches pre-algebra reasoning skills beginning in kindergarten, said that students from other states are taught these skills in later grades.

A number of teachers and principals also told us that mobile students' records are often not transferred to the new school in a timely way or at all, and, as a result, this can make it difficult for school officials to determine class placement, credit transfer, and the need for special services, such as services related to special education and language proficiency. Several teachers said that when students arrive without records, the school must observe and document whether students need special education services—a process that is very comprehensive and can take several weeks or months. In an effort to help schools make more informed decisions about class placement and identification of students with special needs, Texas has developed a system to electronically transfer student records between schools in the state. This system allows schools to share information on what classes students took at the previous school, their grades and standardized test scores, reasons for withdrawal, annual absences, immunization records, and special circumstances, such as English proficiency, migrant status, homeless status, participation in gifted programs or special education, whether the student has an Individualized Education Program,[16] and eligibility for NSLP.

Schools also face the challenge of helping mobile students adjust socially and emotionally to the new school environment. While some students adjust well to their new school, some do not. A few teachers, principals, and other school officials said that some mobile students may feel like they do not belong, fail to make new friends, exhibit poor attendance, and, in some cases, drop out. Others who have difficulty fitting in socially may try to gain attention by exhibiting certain behavior, such as disrupting other students in the class. Also, some guidance counselors and teachers told us some mobile students often act detached, especially when they have changed schools repeatedly and anticipate changing again. In some of the schools we visited, new students were paired with a "buddy" who walks them to class, sits with them at lunch, and helps them learn classroom routines and procedures. Some schools also provided orientation tours of the school for new students and parents and arranged for new students to meet with the guidance counselor to help with the transition. For example, in a suburban/rural public school district in Michigan we visited, the principal and teachers at the elementary school meet with new students and their parents on the first day of the school year; students officially start school the next day. This gives advance notice to teachers about incoming students and allows them time to prepare. In addition, the junior high school in this district has a welcoming committee to introduce new students and parents to the school faculty and provide a tour of the school.

Several school officials told us that the needs of mobile and nonmobile students can extend beyond the classroom and often their families are in need of services too. To help address the family circumstances that contribute to mobility, two school districts we visited use school-based family resource centers that rely on partnerships between the school, community, church, and city agencies to arrange for "wraparound" services for the entire family—such as services related to housing, employment and finances, health care, education for parents and children, and social support networks. In all three states we visited, some schools have specific school-based or community outreach to parents that can benefit both mobile and nonmobile families, such as parenting classes on a range of topics, like budgeting and accessing housing. Also, homeless students, who are often mobile, may lack basic supplies, for example, backpacks, school supplies, and school uniforms, and they may miss school frequently because of issues such as lack of transportation or domestic violence. In addition, some school officials told us they help arrange for services for homeless mobile students and their families, such as coordinating with local homeless shelters and arranging to provide homeless mobile students with food on the weekends when they do not have access to free breakfast and lunch at school.

SCHOOLS USE A RANGE OF FEDERAL PROGRAMS ALREADY IN PLACE TO MEET THE NEEDS OF MOBILE STUDENTS

Because the highly mobile schools we visited also had large percentages of low-income, disadvantaged students and special populations already targeted by federal programs, the schools met the needs of mobile students using funding from programs already in place. For example, during our site visits, a number of school officials and state and local educational agency officials told us they relied on funds from Title I, Part A of ESEA, a federal program targeted to disadvantaged students, including those who are from low-income families, have limited English proficiency, are from migrant families, have disabilities, or are neglected or delinquent. Services available under Title I, Part A are intended to ensure that disadvantaged children have a fair and equal opportunity to obtain a high-quality education and to reach proficiency on assessments based on the state's academic standards.[17] Some school officials and state and local educational agency officials told us they used funds from Title I, Part A to pay for tutoring, after-school instruction, teachers' salaries, technology upgrades, school field trips, and staff development and training on addressing diverse needs of mobile and nonmobile students. One school we visited used funding provided by the American Recovery and Reinvestment Act of 2009 (Recovery Act)[18] for ESEA Title I, Part A to, among other things, hire additional teachers to provide small-group instruction to all students who are behind academically, including mobile students. See table 1 for information about school-based federal programs for disadvantaged and special needs students.

School officials in one district we visited told us that some of their mobile students are eligible for services under the Individuals with Disabilities Education Act, a program that provides early intervention and special education services for children and youths with disabilities.[19] The schools we visited also received funding through the Department of Agriculture's school nutrition programs,[20] which provide free and reduced-price school meals for low-income, disadvantaged students. School officials in some locations said that this program allows them to provide school meals to a large percentage of their student body, including both mobile and nonmobile students.

In addition, some schools we visited used the McKinney-Vento Education for Homeless Children and Youth Program (McKinney-Vento Program),[21] which is designed to meet the educational needs of homeless students. Some school officials told us that homeless students are often mobile. Specifically, the McKinney-Vento Program requires all school districts to put in place homeless education liaisons. Some homeless education liaisons and other school officials we interviewed said they used funds from the McKinney-Vento Program to provide homeless students with food, clothing, school uniforms, backpacks of toiletries and school supplies, tutoring at homeless shelters, academic enrichment services, and summer programs. The McKinney-Vento Program also requires all school districts to provide transportation to those homeless students who choose to remain in their school of origin,[22] however funding for transportation is provided by the school district. Some schools we visited used their own school funds to pay for transportation, such as bus passes and gas cards, as needed, for homeless students to get to school. Schools we visited also used McKinney-Vento Program funds for various other purposes, including one school that used the funds to hire staff to identify homeless students and two other schools that used the funds to provide outreach to parents. Across all three states we visited, homeless education liaisons help provide a stable environment for homeless students to learn by arranging for services for their families, such as referrals to soup kitchens, health services including free dental clinics, free school supplies, and domestic violence groups.

According to state education agency officials we interviewed, schools in their states relied on the Migrant Education Program, which supports the educational needs of a specific population of mobile students—students who are migrant workers or children of migrant parents.[23] The Migrant Education Program (1) provides students with services, such as academic (tutoring and summer school) and health services; (2) allows school districts to share migrant student information electronically across state boundaries; (3) encourages states to collaborate in administering state assessments and sharing lesson plans; and (4) provides funding for "portable" education services, such as instructional booklets and CD-ROM learning modules that help migrant students earn school credits as they move from school to school or undergo extended absences.

Table 1. School-based Federal Programs That Serve Disadvantaged and Other Special Needs Students, Including Mobile Students

Federal agency implementing program	Name of law or program	Purpose of program	Population served by program	Funding for program
Department of Education	Title I, Part A of ESEA	To ensure that disadvantaged children have a fair and equal opportunity to obtain a high-quality education and to reach proficiency on assessments based on state academic standards.	Disadvantaged students, including children who are low-income, limited English proficient, migratory, children with disabilities, or neglected or delinquent.	• Formula-based distribution • Regular: $14.5 billion (fiscal year 2009) • Recovery Act: $10 billion (fiscal year 2009)
	McKinney-Vento Education for Homeless Children and Youth Program	To ensure that homeless students have equal access to free, appropriate public education as other children and youth.	Homeless children and youth.	• Formula-based distribution; funds disseminated through a state-run grant process • Regular: $65.4 million (fiscal year 2009) • Recovery Act: $70 million (fiscal year 2009)
	Migrant Education Program	To ensure that migrant children fully benefit from the same free public education provided to other children.	Migrant students in the agricultural and fishing sectors.	• Formula-based distribution based on each state's count of eligible migratory children and per-pupil expenditure • Regular: $394.8million (fiscal year 2009)
	Individuals with Disabilities Education Act	To provide early intervention, special education, and related services to children and	Students with disabilities.	• Formula-based grants to states based on the number of students receiving special education services

Federal agency implementing program	Name of law or program	Purpose of program	Population served by program	Funding for program
		youths with disabilities.		<ul><li>Regular: $23.8billion (fiscal year 2010)</li><li>Recovery Act: $11.3billion in grants to states (fiscal year 2009)</li></ul>
Department of Agriculture	School Breakfast Program (SBP) and NSLP	To provide nutritionally-balanced free or reduced price breakfasts and lunches to low-income students.	Low-income students.	<ul><li>Cash reimbursements and direct food donations</li><li>Regular: $9 billion (NSLP) and $2.6 billion (SBP) (fiscal year 2009)</li><li>Recovery Act: $100 million (fiscal year 2009)</li></ul>
Department of Health and Human Services	Head Start	To promote school readiness by enhancing the social and cognitive development of children through the provision of educational, health, nutritional, social and other services to economically disadvantaged children and families.	Low-income children age 0-5.	<ul><li>Grants to local public and private organizations</li><li>Regular: $5 billion (fiscal year 2009)</li><li>Recovery Act: $2.1 billion(fiscal year 2009)</li></ul>

Sources: GAO analysis of information from the Departments of Education, Agriculture, and Health and Human Services.

Note: GAO did not independently verify the information in this table.

| 74 | United States Government Accountability Office |

States use the Migrant Student Information Exchange—a Web-based database—to collect, maintain, and share student record infor-mation to facilitate school enrollment, grade and course placement, and accrual of secondary school course credits.[24]

We did not evaluate the effective-ness of these federal programs in meeting the needs of mobile students.

We provided a draft copy of this report to the Department of Education for review and comment. Education did not have any comments on the report.

Cornelia M. Ashby
Director, Education, Workforce, and Income Security Issues

APPENDIX I: SCOPE AND METHODOLOGY

This appendix discusses in more detail our methodology for our study examining the scope and implications of student mobility on students and schools. Our study was framed around four questions: (1) What are the numbers and characteristics of students who change schools, and what are the reasons students change schools? (2) What is known about the effects of mobility on student outcomes including academic achievement, behavior, and other outcomes? (3) What challenges does student mobility present for schools in meeting the educational needs of students who change schools? (4) What key federal programs are schools using to address the needs of mobile students?

Analysis of Federal Datasets

To obtain information on the number and characteristics of mobile students and schools they attend, we analyzed two nationally representative datasets that are administered by the Department of Education's (Education) National Center for Education Statistics (NCES)—the *Early Childhood Longitudinal Study, Kindergarten Class of 1998-1 999* (ECLS-K) and the *National Assessment of Educational Progress* (NAEP). We selected these datasets in consultation with our methodologists and Education officials.

For both datasets, we assessed the quality, reliability, and usability of the data for reporting descriptive statistics on the characteristics of students and the schools they attend. For our data reliability assessment, we reviewed agency documents about the datasets' variable definitions, survey and sampling methods, and data collection and analysis efforts. We also conducted electronic tests of the files and interviewed Education officials about the steps they took to ensure data reliability. We determined that the Education data were sufficiently reliable for the purposes of our review. The surveys used weighted probability sampling of students (ECLS-K) and schools (NAEP). We followed recommended statistical techniques to estimate standard errors of estimates from the ECLS-K and NAEP data.

The ECLS-K's measure of individual-level student mobility is limited in that its measure of school changes includes the number of promotional school changes—for example, the typical school change from an elementary school to a middle school—as well as the nonpromotional school changes.

Early Childhood Longitudinal Survey, Kindergarten Class of 1998-1999

The ECLS-K is a longitudinal survey of students from kindergarten through eighth grade. The survey population is a nationally representative cohort of 21,260 students who began kindergarten in 1998. The survey collects data from students, parents, teachers, and school officials from 1998 to 2007. In our analysis of ECLS-K data, we focused on the eighth grade survey round, to ensure that we captured the most complete data on school changes.

During each spring survey round from first through eighth grade, parents were asked how many times their child changed schools since the last survey period. We used the responses from those questions, as well as school identification information, to estimate the number of school changes for each student. We examined the following student characteristics available in the ECLS-K data: (1) race; (2) measures of family income, including poverty threshold, receipt of free or reduced- price lunch, food stamps, or assistance from the Temporary Assistance for Needy Families (TANF) program; (3) whether a father was present in the household; and (4) whether the family owned their home.

We compared students who changed schools two or fewer times (referred to as "less mobile") to those who changed schools four or more times (referred to as "more mobile"). We chose those groups for comparison because they provide a clear separation between the more mobile and less mobile groups and also because the two groups combined represent a significant fraction—about 82 percent—of the population of the students in the cohort. Students who changed schools four or more times would generally have experienced at least three nonpromotional school moves. We also considered defining high

76   United States Government Accountability Office

mobility students as those who changed five or more times. However, such students only made up about 5 percent of the population followed by the ECLS-K. Because table cell sample sizes were often very small using the five change cut-off, resulting in wide confidence intervals, we decided against the use of this definition.

In addition to the analyses we presented in the main body of this report, we compared students who changed schools two or fewer times to those who changed schools three or more times. We found statistically significant differences among some of the relationships we explored, but as expected, the differences were more pronounced when the highly mobile population was defined as students who changed four or more times. See appendix II for ECLS-K data on the mobile student population.

National Assessment of Educational Progress

The NAEP—the results of which are issued as the Nation's Report Card—provides nationally representative results on school characteristics based on samples of 4th, 8th, and 12th grade students.[25] Similar to our analysis of the ECLS-K, our analysis of NAEP focused on the eighth grade year. We used the results from survey questions related to school environment and characteristics to describe the characteristics of schools and their student mobility rates. To determine schools' student mobility rates, we used responses from the following question administered in the 2007 survey: "About what percentage of students who are enrolled at the beginning of the school year is still enrolled at the end of the school year?"[26] Further, using the NAEP data, we explored relationships between schools' mobility rates and the following school characteristics: (1) geographic location; (2) measures of low-income students, such as receipt of Elementary and Secondary Education Act of 1965's (ESEA) Title I funding[27] and participation in the National School Lunch Program (NSLP);[28] (3) students in special education; (4) students with limited English proficiency; and (5) students absent on an average day.

For our comparison of schools with "low" student mobility rates and schools with "high" student mobility rates, we sorted the NAEP data into three pairings to determine which pairing provided a clear separation between low mobility and high mobility schools. When we compared schools that had 5 percent or fewer of their students no longer enrolled at the end of the school year (low mobility) with schools that had more than 5 percent of their students no longer enrolled at the end of the year (high mobility), we found few statistically significant differences. When we compared schools that had 10 percent or fewer of their students no longer enrolled at the end of the school year (low mobility) with schools that had more than 10 percent of their students no longer enrolled at the end of the year (high mobility), we found several statistical differences. When we compared schools that had 20 percent or fewer of their students no longer enrolled at the end of the school year (low mobility) with schools that had more than 20 percent of their students no longer enrolled at the end of the year (high mobility), cell sample sizes were too small to make meaningful comparisons. We thus selected the 10 percent pairing because it provides a clear separation between the low mobility and high mobility schools and the sample sizes were sufficient to make meaningful comparisons. See appendix III for NAEP data on schools.

Review of External Research Studies

We reviewed existing studies to determine what research says about the effects of mobility on student outcomes, including academic and nonacademic outcomes, such as behavior. To identify existing studies, we searched several electronic databases using the keywords "student mobility," "school mobility," and "transience."[29] We identified 151 studies that met the following criteria:

- original analysis of data based on students in the United States or original quantitative synthesis of such previously conducted research (also referred to as meta-analysis[30]) and
- published or prepared during or after 1984.

We screened the studies to identify those that were relevant for our study and identified 62 of the 151 studies that met the following criteria:

- assessed a student's school change as distinct from a student's residential change;
- used quantitative measurement of the association between school change and at least one student outcome, either academic or non-academic; and
- peer-reviewed journal article, association or agency paper, state or local education agency paper, or a conference paper from the last 2 years (2007 onward).

Each of these 62 studies was reviewed by a social scientist to determine whether the study (1) contained sufficient information on methods to make a determination about the study's soundness and limitations and (2) for studies on academic outcomes only—controlled for students' academic performance prior to changing schools. For the purpose of controlling, we considered a variety of methods to be sufficient, such as

- using a statistical model that included prior academic performance as a predictor or covariate,
- matching students on prior performance, or
- analyzing difference scores (i.e., difference between premobility academic performance and postmobility performance) rather than absolute measures of achievement.

The result of this stage of the review was a set of studies that we determined used sound methods and, in the case of studies of academic outcomes, controlled for prior academic achievement. For each of these studies, we also reviewed the other studies these authors used as references, screened these studies using the same methods described above, and identified one additional study that met our inclusion criteria. Further, we excluded a few studies due to redundancy (covering the same or nearly the same data and analysis as other studies included in the review). At the end of the screening process, 26 studies on the effects of mobility on student outcomes remained, of which 21 assessed academic outcomes and 11 assessed nonacademic outcomes.[31]

To review the findings, methods, and limitations of the selected studies, we developed a data collection instrument to obtain information systematically about each study's methods, findings, and limitations on the reliability, scope, and generalizability of these findings. We based our data collection and assessments on generally accepted social science standards. A senior social scientist with training in survey methods and statistical analysis of survey data reviewed each study using the data collection instrument. A second senior social scientist reviewed each completed data collection instrument and the relevant portions of the study in question to verify the accuracy of the information recorded. Most of our selected studies measured academic outcomes using standardized test scores or school dropout or completion rates and nonacademic outcomes using misbehavior and social capital (i.e., richness of students' social networks).

We selected the studies for our review based on their methodological soundness and not on the generalizability of the results. Although the findings of the studies we identified are not representative of the findings of all studies of student mobility, the studies consist of those published studies we could identify that used the strongest designs to assess the effects of mobility. The selected studies varied in methods and in scope. For example, some studies distinguished among types of mobility (e.g., intra-city versus city-to-suburbs, or school-change-only versus schoolchange-plus-residential-move), but others did not. Some studies used nationally representative samples of students, while others focused on specific populations, such as low-income students in one city. Some studies assessed effects of mobility at the student level, while others assessed effects at higher levels, such as classrooms. See appendix IV for a list of the studies we reviewed.

School Site Visits

We conducted site visits to a nonprobability sample of eight schools across six school districts in three states (California, Michigan, and Texas) where we interviewed school officials and others about issues related to student mobility. We selected states that provided geographic coverage and that had high percentages of economically disadvantaged students and/or high rates of foreclosures to provide insight on how the economic downturn might be affecting students and schools in high poverty areas. We selected schools with high percentages of mobile students and that would illustrate school type (public and charter), grade level (elementary, middle, and high school), and location (urban, suburban, and rural).

During our school site visits, we interviewed state education agency officials, local homeless education liaisons, principals, teachers, guidance counselors, school social workers, community group representatives, and parents of mobile students. During our interviews, we collected information about

- the number and demographic characteristics of mobile students;
- reasons for student mobility and timing of mobility;
- challenges related to student mobility, including meeting academic, social, and emotional needs of mobile and nonmobile students; and

80 United States Government Accountability Office

- how schools address challenges of student mobility, including use of federal programs and community resources.

In preparation for our site visits, we reviewed relevant laws, regulations, and agency documents, and interviewed federal officials and representatives of education and homeless associations about issues related to student mobility and federal programs that serve low-income, disadvantaged, and special needs students, including those who change schools.

We conducted this performance audit from October 2009 through November 2010 in accordance with generally accepted government auditing standards. Those standards require that we plan and perform the audit to obtain sufficient, appropriate evidence to provide a reasonable basis for our findings and conclusions based on our audit objectives. We believe that the evidence obtained provides a reasonable basis for our findings and conclusions based on our audit objectives.

APPENDIX II: DATA ON CHARACTERISTICS OF MOBILE STUDENT POPULATIONS

This appendix provides information from the *Early Childhood Longitudinal Study, Kindergarten Class of 1998-1999* (ECLS-K)—which followed a cohort of students from 1998 to 2007—on the number of schools students attended, by various student and parent characteristics

Table 2. Number of Times Students Changed Schools by Eighth Grade

Number of school changes	Percentage of students who changed schools
0	5%
1	31
2	34
3	18
4 or more	13

Source: ECLS-K data, 1998-2007.

Note: Data derived from interviews of parents who were asked in each survey round a version of the question: "Since spring 2004 how many times has your child changed from one school to another?"

. In each table, we provide a comparison of the percent of students who changed schools two times or less to students who changed schools three or more times, and students who changed schools four or more times.

Table 3. Percent of Students from Families with Incomes below the Poverty Level

Number of school changes	Percent of students from families with incomes below the poverty level
Comparison between 2 or less versus 3 or more school changes	
2 or less	17%
3 or more	22[a]
Comparison between 2 or less versus 4 or more school changes	
2 or less	17
4 or more	26[a]

Source: ECLS-K data, 1998-2007.

Note: Data derived by combining data on household income and the number of people living in the household with estimates of the poverty threshold published by the Census Bureau.

[a] Indicates differences between the comparisons were statistically significant at the 95 percent confidence level.

Table 4. Percent of Students from Families Receiving TANF

Number of school changes	Percent of students from families receiving TANF
Comparison between 2 or less versus 3 or more school changes	
2 or less	3%
3or more	6[a]
Comparison between 2 or less versus 4 or more school changes	
2 or less	3
4 or more	9[a]

Source: ECLS-K data, 1998-2007.

Note: Data derived from interviews of parents who were asked: "In the past 12 months, have you or anyone in your household received Temporary Assistance for Needy Families?"

[a] Indicates differences between the comparisons were statistically significant at the 95 percent confidence level.

Table 5. Percent of Students Receiving Free or Reduced-Price Lunch

Number of school changes	Percent of students receiving free or reduced-price lunch
Comparison between 2 or less versus 3 or more school changes	
2 or less	40%
3or more	49[a]
Comparison between 2 or less versus 4 or more school changes	
2 or less	40
4 or more	54[a]

Source: ECLS-K data, 1998-2007.

Note: Data derived from interviews of parents who were asked: "Does your child receive free or reduced-price lunches at school?"

[a] Indicates differences between the comparisons were statistically significant at the 95 percent confidence level.

Table 6. Percent of Students From Families Receiving Food Stamps

Number of school changes	Percent of students whose families receive food stamps
Comparison between 2 or less versus 3 or more school changes	
2 or less	11%
3 or more	18[a]
Comparison between 2 or less versus 4 or more school changes	
2 or less	11
4 or more	25[a]

Source: ECLS-K data, 1998-2007.

Note: Data derived from interviews of parents who were asked: "In the past 12 months, have you or anyone in your household received food stamps?

[a] Indicates differences between the comparisons were statistically significant at the 95 percent confidence level.

Table 7. Percent of Students with No Father in the Household

Number of school changes	Percent of students with no father in the household
Comparison between 2 or less versus 3 or more school changes	
2 or less	21%
3 or more	28[a]
Comparison between 2 or less versus 4 or more school changes	
2 or less	21
4 or more	31[a]

Source: ECLS-K data, 1998-2007.

Note: Father's presence was determined by ECLS-K surveyor during interviews of parents.

[a] Indicates differences between the comparisons were statistically significant at the 95 percent confidence level.

Table 8. Percent of Students of Various Races

Number of school changes	Percent of students classified as Black or African-American, Non-Hispanic students	Percent of students classified as Hispanic	Percent of students classified as White	Percent of students classified as other
Comparison between 2 or less versus 3 or more school changes				
2 or less	15%	18%	60%	7%
3 or more	21[a]	18	53[a]	8
Comparison between 2 or less versus 4 or more school changes				
2 or less	15	18	60	7
4 or more	23[b]	18	51[b]	8

Source: ECLS-K data, 1998-2007.

Note: Data derived from interviews of parents who were given various racial or ethnic categories to indicate their child's race.

[a] Indicates differences between the comparisons were statistically significant at the 95 percent confidence level.

[b] Indicates differences between the comparisons were statistically significant at the 90 percent confidence level.

84 United States Government Accountability Office

Table 9. Percent of Students from Families Who Do Not Own Their Home

Number of school changes	Percent of students from families that do not own their home
Comparison between 2 or less versus 3 or more school changes	
2 or less	20%
3 or more	32[a]
Comparison between 2 or less versus 4 or more school changes	
2 or less	20
4 or more	39[a]

Source: ECLS-K data, 1998-2007.

Note: Data derived from interviews of parents who were asked: "Do you [or anyone else in your family living there] own the home or apartment, pay rent, or do something else?"

[a] Indicates differences between the comparisons were statistically significant at the 95 percent confidence level.

APPENDIX III: DATA ON CHARACTERISTICS OF SCHOOLS REGARDING MOBILE STUDENT POPULATIONS

This appendix includes data from the *National Assessment of Educational Progress* (NAEP), which is also known as the Nation's Report Card. The NAEP is a continuing assessment of student progress conducted nationwide periodically in reading, math, science, writing, U.S. history, civics, geography, and the arts. The NAEP assessment collects data from students and school officials for a nationally representative sample of 4th, 8th, and 12th graders. In the following tables, we present data on the characteristics of students in grades four and eight from the 2007 NAEP assessment for schools with "low" and "high" mobility rates. Schools with low mobility rates had fewer than 10 percent of their students who were no longer enrolled at the end of the year while schools with high mobility rates had more than 10 percent of their students who were no longer enrolled at the end of the school year. The tables are based on a selection of variables relevant to our review.

Table 10. Mobility by Geographic Region of Schools

Region	4th grade				8th grade			
	Schools with low mobility		Schools with high mobility		Schools with low mobility		Schools with high mobility	
	Number of schools	Percent	Number of schools	Percent	Number of schools	Percent	Number of schools	Percent
Northeast	9,870.7	20.08%	885.7	7.68%	6,542.9	20.66%	365.7	8.90%
Midwest	14,163.9	28.81	2,281.2	19.78	9,143.1	28.87[a]	1,014.7	24.69[a]
South	15,597.9	31.72	4,273.8	37.05	10,135.1	32.00[a]	1,345.7	32.75[a]
West	9,534.7	19.39	4,094.6	35.50	5,851.1	18.47	1,383.2	33.66
Total	**49,167.2**	**100%**	**11,535.2**	**100%**	**31,672.3**	**100%**	**4,109.3**	**100%**

Source: GAO analysis of NAEP data, 2007.

[a] Indicates differences between schools with low mobility and schools with high mobility were not statistically significant at the 95 percent confidence level.

Table 11. Mobility by Metro-Centric Type of Locale

Metro-centric type of locale	4th grade				8th grade			
	Schools with low mobility		Schools with high mobility		Schools with low mobility		Schools with high mobility	
	Number of schools	Percent	Number of schools	Percent	Number of schools	Percent	Number of schools	Percent
Large city	7,182.3	14.61%	2,238.0	19.40%	4,269.3	13.48%	771.8	18.78%
Midsize city	6,156.0	12.52	2,608.9	22.62	3,867.6	12.21	696.8	16.96
Urban fringe of large city	12,305.4	25.03[a]	2,666.4	23.12[a]	6,898.1	21 .78[a]	862.6	20.99[a]
Urban fringe or midsize	5,631.2	11.45[a]	1,159.3	10.05[a]	3,417.9	10.79[a]	453.1	11.03[a]

Table 11. (Continued)

Metro-centric type of locale	4th grade				8th grade			
	Schools with low mobility		Schools with high mobility		Schools with low mobility		Schools with high mobility	
	Number of schools	Percent	Number of schools	Percent	Number of schools	Percent	Number of schools	Percent
Large town	609.3	1.24[a]	162.0	1.40[a]	241.7	0.76[a]	45.9	1.12[a]
Small town	3,302.2	6.72[a]	897.1	7.78[a]	2,433.0	7.68[a]	348.1	8.47[a]
Rural	7,804.3	15.87	896.8	7.77	6,126.9	19.34	433.2	10.54
Rural, inside Core Based Statistical Area	6,176.4	12.56	906.7	7.86	4,417.6	13.95[a]	497.8	12.11a
Total	49,167.2	100%	11,535.2	100%	31,672.3	100%	4,109.3	100%

Source: GAO analysis of NAEP data, 2007.

[a] Indicates differences between schools with low mobility and schools with high mobility were not statistically significant at the 95 percent confidence level.

Table 12. Mobility by Receipt of Title I Funding

Received Title I funding	4th grade				8th grade			
	Schools with low mobility		Schools with high mobility		Schools with low mobility		Schools with high mobility	
	Number of schools	Percent	Number of schools	Percent	Number of schools	Percent	Number of schools	Percent
No	20,207.9	41.28%	2,020.5	17.53%	16,727.8	53.63%	1,555.2	37.99%
Yes, for students	15,635.6	31.94	1,993.8	17.30	7,809.3	25.04	691.4	16.89
Yes, for school purpose	13,105.9	26.77	7,509.8	65.17	6,651.8	21.33	1,847.3	45.12
Total	48,949.4	100%	11,524.1	100%	31,188.9	100%	4,094.0	100%

Source: GAO analysis of NAEP data, 2007.

Table 13. Mobility by Percent of Students Receiving Targeted Title I Services

Percent of students receiving targeted Title I services	4th grade				8th grade			
	Schools with low mobility		Schools with high mobility		Schools with low mobility		Schools with high mobility	
	Number of schools	Percent	Number of schools	Percent	Number of schools	Percent	Number of schools	Percent
None	22,790.2	48.72%	4,224.6	38.79%	18,198.4	60.71%	1,905.4	50.03%
1-5%	3,818.8	8.16	206.6	1.90	2,836.0	9.46	45.6	1.20
6-10	4,525.1	9.67	498.9	4.58	2,163.4	7.22	135.5	3.56
11-25	6,512.3	13.92[a]	1,241.7	11.40[a]	2,284.8	7.62[a]	246.5	6.47[a]
26-50	3,084.6	6.59	1,082.5	9.94	1,541.8	5.14[a]	249.4	6.55[a]
51-75	796.5	1.70	677.3	6.22	533.2	1.78	287.6	7.55
76-90	810.8	1.73	476.2	4.37	335.9	1.12	173.8	4.56
More than 90	4,444.4	9.50	2,482.9	22.80	2,083.1	6.95	764.3	20.07
Total sample	**46,782.6**	**100%**	**10,890.9**	**100%**	**29,976.6**	**100%**	**3,808.1**	**100%**

Source: GAO analysis of NAEP data, 2007.

[a] Indicates differences between schools with low mobility and schools with high mobility were *not* statistically significant at the 95 percent confidence level.

Table 14. Mobility by Students Eligible for NSLP

Percent of students eligible for NSLP	4th grade				8th grade			
	Schools with low mobility		Schools with high mobility		Schools with low mobility		Schools with high mobility	
	Number of schools	Percent	Number of schools	Percent	Number of schools	Percent	Number of schools	Percent
0-10%	8,237.3	21.54%	158.0	1.44%	4,748.1	21.48%	47.4	1.25%
11-25	6,146.0	16.07	426.1	3.89	3,838.5	17.36	165.7	4.38
26-34	4,066.9	10.64	576.5	5.26	2,152.7	9.74[a]	278.2	7.34[a]
35-50	6,338.8	16.58[a]	1,690.4	15.43[a]	3,968.2	17.95[a]	652.7	17.23[a]
51-75	7,060.1	18.47	3,850.6	35.15	3,872.1	17.52	1,100.0	29.04
76-99	5,234.5	13.69	3,754.6	34.28	2,879.9	13.03	1,172.1	30.95
100	1,150.9	3.01[a]	497.1	4.54[a]	647.9	2.93	371.5	9.81
Total	38,234.5	100%	10,953.4	100%	22,107.3	100%	3,787.6	100%

Source: GAO analysis of NAEP data, 2007.

[a] Indicates differences between schools with low mobility and schools with high mobility were *not* statistically significant at the 95 percent confidence level.

Table 15. Mobility by How Schools Administer the NSLP

Determine eligibility for NSLP	Schools with low mobility		Schools with high mobility		Schools with low mobility		Schools with high mobility	
	Number of schools	Percent	Number of schools	Percent	Number of schools	Percent	Number of schools	Percent
By individual student	35,708.7	96.03%	10,031.4	91.59%	2,0312	95.15%	3,373.7	89.95%
By special provisions	1,478.2	3.97	920.7	8.41	1,034.3	4.85	377.0	10.05
Total	37,186.8	100%	10,952.1	100%	21,346.3	100%	3,750.7	100%

Source: GAO analysis of NAEP data, 2007.

Table 16. Mobility by School Participation in the NSLP

School in NSLP	4th grade				8th grade			
	Schools with low mobility		Schools with high mobility		Schools with low mobility		Schools with high mobility	
	Number of schools	Percent	Number of schools	Percent	Number of schools	Percent	Number of schools	Percent
Yes	37,092.8	75.87%	10,889.0	94.89%	21,276.4	67.66%	3741.8	91.42%
No	11,794.5	24.13	586.4	5.11	10,170.6	32.34	351.2	8.58
Total	**48,887.3**	**100%**	**11,475.4**	**100%**	**31,447.0**	**100%**	**4,093.0**	**100%**

Source: GAO analysis of NAEP data, 2007.

Table 17. Mobility by Special Education Students

Percent of special education students	4th grade				8th grade			
	Schools with low mobility		Schools with high mobility		Schools with low mobility		Schools with high mobility	
	Number of schools	Percent	Number of schools	Percent	Number of schools	Percent	Number of schools	Percent
0-5%	18,426.2	38.98%	1,690.2	15.10%	13,092.9	43.39%	393.8	9.78%
6-10	13,220.3	27.97[a]	3,504.8	31.30[a]	6,137.6	20.34[a]	965.7	23.98[a]
11-25	14,016.2	29.65	5,449.5	48.67	9,518.4	31.54	2,003.0	49.73
26-50	1,230.7	2.60	493.0	4.40	1,015.8	3.37	320.6	7.96
51-100	375.4	0.79[a]	58.6	0.52[a]	411.2	1.36	344.3	8.55
Total	**47,268.7**	**100%**	**11,196.1**	**100%**	**30,175.8**	**100%**	**4,027.5**	**100%**

Source: GAO analysis of NAEP data, 2007.

[a] Indicates differences between schools with low mobility and schools with high mobility were *not* statistically significant at the 95 percent confidence level.

Table 18. Mobility by Students Who are Limited English Proficient

Percent of students with limited English proficiency	4th grade				8th grade			
	Schools with low mobility		Schools with high mobility		Schools with low mobility		Schools with high mobility	
	Number of schools	Percent	Number of schools	Percent	Number of schools	Percent	Number of schools	Percent
0%	21,648.8	44.65%	1,954.3	17.07%	16,574.7	53.32%	1,288.8	32.02%
1-5	16,098.5	33.20	2,919.3	25.50	10,193.6	32.79[a]	1,159.6	28.81[a]
6-10	3,325.9	6.86	1,164.9	10.17	1,672.3	5.38	419.9	10.43
11-25	3,732.5	7.70	2,282.0	19.93	1,571.3	5.05	577.8	14.35
26-50	2,074.6	4.28	1,904.8	16.64	717.9	2.31	449.7	11.17
51-75	808.6	1.67	848.8	7.41	239.7	0.77	106.9	2.66
76-100	794.3	1.64[a]	375.2	3.28[a]	116.3	0.37[a]	22.9	0.57[a]
Total	**48,483.1**	**100%**	**11,449.3**	**100%**	**31,085.7**	**100%**	**4,025.7**	**100%**

Source: GAO analysis of NAEP data, 2007.

[a] Indicates differences between schools with low mobility and schools with high mobility were *not* statistically significant at the 95 percent confidence level.

Table 19. Mobility by Percent of Students Absent on an Average Day

Percent absent	4th grade				8th grade			
	Schools with low mobility		Schools with high mobility		Schools with low mobility		Schools with high mobility	
	Number of schools	Percent	Number of schools	Percent	Number of schools	Percent	Number of schools	Percent
0-2%	20,059.5	41.34%	2,029.0	17.65%	13,398.7	42.94%	721.0	17.68%
3-5	25,153.9	51.84	6,817.6	59.32	14,292.5	45.80[a]	1,805.1	44.25[a]
6-10	3,043.1	6.27	2,461.4	21.42	3,323.2	10.65	1,210.5	29.67
More than 10	266.2	0.55	185.8	1.62	191.3	0.61	342.6	8.40
Total	48,522.7	100%	11,493.8	100%	31,205.7	100%	4,079.2	100%

Source: GAO analysis of NAEP data, 2007.

[a] Indicates differences between schools with low mobility and schools with high mobility were *not* statistically significant at the 95 percent confidence level.

Appendix IV: Literature Review of Published Research on Student Mobility

This appendix includes studies of possible academic and nonacademic outcomes of student mobility that met our criteria for inclusion in our review.

Study title	Author and source	Grade levels or ages	Geographic or demographic scope	Type of student outcomes[a]
Children in Motion: School Transfers and Elementary School Performance	Alexander, Karl L., Doris R. Entwisle, and Susan L. Dauber. *The Journal of Educational Research*, vol. 90, no. 1 (September/October 1996): 3-12.	Grades 1-5	District/city (Baltimore); urban, poor (data were intended to be representative of all Baltimore schoolchildren, but attrition over the 5 years of the study resulted in bias towards a African-American, low-socio-economic status (SES) population)	Academic
The Impact of Charter School Attendance on Student Performance	Booker, Kevin et al. *Journal of Public Economics*, vol. 91 (2007): 849-876.	Grade 4	State (Texas)	Academic
School Mobility in the Early Elementary Grades: Frequency and Impact From	Burkam, David T., Valerie E. Lee, and Julie Dwyer. Prepared for the Workshop on the Impact of Mobility and Change on the Lives	Kindergarten through grade 3	National	Academic

Study title	Author and source	Grade levels or ages	Geographic or demographic scope	Type of student outcomes[a]
Nationally-Representative Data	of Young Children, Schools, and Neighborhoods (June 29-30, 2009).			
Disruption Versus Tiebout Improvement: The Costs and Benefits of Switching Schools	Hanushek, Eric A., John F. Kain, and Steven G. Rivkin. *Journal of Public Economics*, vol. 88(2004): 1721-1746.	Grades 4-7	State (Texas)	Academic
School Mobility and Student Achievement in an Urban Setting	Heinlein, Lisa Melman, and Marybeth Shinn. *Psychology in the Schools*, vol. 37, no. 4 (2000): 349-357.	Kindergarten through grade 6	District/city (New York City community); urban, largely minority and low-income population	Academic
Head Start Children: School Mobility and Achievement in the Early Grades	Mantzicopoulos, Panayota, and Dana J. Knutson. *The Journal of Educational Research*, vol. 93, no. 5 (May/June 2000): 305-311.	Kindergarten through grade 2	District/city (Midwestern community); suburban, economically disadvantaged, prior Head Start attendees	Academic
Student Mobility, Academic Performance, and School Accountability	Mao, Michael X., Maria D. Whitsett, and Lynn T. Mellor. Paper presented at the Annual Meeting of the American Educational Research Association, Chicago (Mar 24-28,1997).	Grades 1-8	State (Texas)	Academic

Appendix IV: (Continued)

Study title	Author and source	Grade levels or ages	Geographic or demographic scope	Type of student outcomes[a]
Predictors of Educational Attainment in the Chicago Longitudinal Study	Ou, Suh-Ruu, and Arthur J. Reynolds. *School PsychologyQuarterly*, vol. 23, no. 2 (2008): 199-229.	Preschool through age 20	District/city (Chicago); urban, low-SES population of mostly African-American children	Academic
Special Education and School Achievement: An Exploratory Analysis	Reynolds, Arthur J., and Barbara Wolfe. *Educational Evaluation and Policy Analysis*,	Kindergarten through grade 6	District/city (Chicago); urban, low-SES population of mostly African-American children	Academic
with a Central-City Sample	vol 21, no. 3(Autumn 1999): 249-269.			
Student Mobility and the Increased Risk of High School Dropout	Rumberger, Russell W., and Katherine A. Larson. *American Journal of Education*, vol. 107, no. 1 (November 1998): 1-35.	Grades 8-12	National	Academic
The Hazards of Changing Schools for California Latino Adolescents	Rumberger, Russell W., Katherine A. Larson, Gregory J. Palardy et al. University of California, Berkeley: Chicano/Latino Policy Project (CLPP) Policy Report, vol. 1, no. 2, (October 1998).	Grades 8-12	State (California)	Academic
The Educational Consequences of	Rumberger, Russell W., Katherine A. Larson, Robert K. Ream et al.	Grades 8-12	State (California)	Academic

Study title	Author and source	Grade levels or ages	Geographic or demographic scope	Type of student outcomes[a]
Mobility for California Students and Schools	University of California, Berkeley and Stanford University: Policy Analysis for California Education Research Series 99-2, (March 1999).			
School Mobility and Achievement: Longitudinal Findings From an Urban Cohort	Temple, Judy A., and Arthur J. Reynolds. *Journal of School Psychology*, vol. 37, no. 4 (1999): 355-377.	Kindergarten through grade 7	District/city (Chicago); urban, low-SES population of mostly African-American children	Academic
Student Transience in North Carolina: The Effect of School Mobility on Student Outcomes Using Longitudinal Data	Xu, Zeyu, Jane Hannaway, and Stephanie D'Souza. National Center for Analysis of Longitudinal Data in Education Research (CALDER) Working Paper no. 22, March 2009.	Grades 3-8	State (North Carolina)	Academic
The Relation of School Structure and Social Environment to Parental Involvement in Elementary Schools	Griffith, James. *The Elementary School Journal*, vol. 99, no. 1 (September 1998): 53-80.	Students in elementary school and parents	District/city; large metropolitan area	Nonacademic

Appendix IV: (Continued)

Study title	Author and source	Grade levels or ages	Geographic or demographic scope	Type of student outcomes[a]
Early Intervention and Juvenile Delinquency Prevention: Evidence from the Chicago	Mann, Emily A., and Arthur J. Reynolds. *Social Work Research*, vol. 30, no. 3(September 2006): 153-167.	Kindergarten through grade 12	District/city (Chicago); urban, low-SES population of mostly African-American children	Nonacademic
Paths of Effects of Early Childhood Intervention on Educational Attainment and Delinquency: A Confirmatory Analysis of the Chicago Child-Parent Centers	Reynolds, Arthur J., Suh-Ruu Ou, and James W. Topitzes. *Child Development*, vol. 75, no. 5 (September/October 2004): 1299-1328.	Kindergarten through age 17	District/city (Chicago); urban, low-SES population of mostly African-American children	Nonacademic
School-Based Early Intervention and Later Child Maltreatment in the Chicago Longitudinal Study	Reynolds, Arthur J., and Dylan L. Robertson. *Child Development*, vol. 74, no. 1 (January/February 2003): 3-26.	Grades 3-7	District/city (Chicago); urban, low-income minority students who participated in school-based early intervention	Nonacademic

Study title	Author and source	Grade levels or ages	Geographic or demographic scope	Type of student outcomes[a]
Friendship Networks of Mobile Adolescents	South, Scott J., and Dana L. Haynie. *Social Forces*, vol 83, no. 1 (September 2004): 315-350.	Grades 7-12 and parents	National	Nonacademic
Longitudinal Effects of Student Mobility on Three Dimensions of Elementary School Engagement	Gruman, Diana H. et al. *Child Development*, vol. 79, no. 6 (November/December 2008): 1833-1852.	Grades 2-5	Schools (10 suburban schools in the Pacific Northwest that had high-risk population of low income, single-family households, high mobility, and poor academic performance)	Academic and nonacademic
Why Are Residential and School Moves Associated with Poor School Performance?	Pribesh, Shana, and Douglas B. Downey. *Demography*, vol. 36, no. 4 (November 1999): 521-534.	Grades 8-12	National	Academic andnonacademic
Toward Understanding How Social Capital Mediates the Impact of Mobility on Mexican American Achievement	Ream, Robert K. *Social Forces*, vol. 84, no. 1 (September 2005): 201-230	Grades 8-12	National; Mexican American students and non-Latino White students	Academic andnonacademic

Study title	Author and source	Grade levels or ages	Geographic or demographic scope	Type of student outcomes[a]
Early Schooling of Children at Risk	Reynolds, Arthur J. *American Educational Research Journal*, vol. 28, no. 2 (Summer 1991): 392-422.	Kindergarten through Grade 2	District/city (Chicago); urban, low-SES population of mostly African-American children	Academic andnonacademic
School Adjustment of Children at Risk Through Fourth Grade	Reynolds, Arthur J., and Nikolaus Bezruczko. *Merrill-Palmer Quarterly*, vol. 39, no. 4 (October 1993): 457-480.	Kindergarten through grade 4	District/city (Chicago); urban, low-SES population of mostly African-American children	Academic andnonacademic
Students on the Move: Residential and Educational Mobility in America's Schools	Swanson, Christopher B., and Barbara Schneider. *Sociology of Education*, vol. 72, no. 1 (January 1999): 54-67.	Grades 8-12	National	Academic andnonacademic

Source: GAO review of existing research.

Note: In addition to the primary research studies included in this table, we reviewed one meta- analysis of studies of academic outcomes of student mobility: Reynolds, A. J., Chen, C.-C., & Herbers, J. E. (June 2009). School Mobility and Educational Success: A Research Synthesis and Evidence on Prevention. Paper presented at the Workshop on the Impact of Mobility and Change on the Lives of Young Children, Schools, and Neighborhoods, National Research Council, Washington, DC.

[a] This column indicates the types of outcomes (academic, nonacademic, or both) for which studies were included in our report. Studies may have included additional outcomes that were not included in our review. For example, a study reviewed for a nonacademic outcome may also have included an academic outcome, but if the study did not control for prior academic achievement, then we would have reviewed the study for its nonacademic outcome only.

United States Government Accountability Office

99

End Notes

[1] We analyzed Education's *Early Childhood Longitudinal Study: Kindergarten Class of 1998-1999* data from 1998-2007 and *National Assessment of Educational Progress* data from 2007.

[2] The McKinney-Vento Homeless Assistance Act requires every local educational agency to designate a liaison who serves as a primary contact between homeless families and schools to help ensure homeless students enroll in school. 42 U.S.C. § 1143 1(g)(6).

[3] GAO, *Elementary School Children: Many Change Schools Frequently, Harming Their Education*, GAO/HEHS-94-45 (Washington, D.C.: Feb. 4, 1994).

[4] Title I, Part A of ESEA provides federal funds to elementary and secondary schools to improve the educational opportunities of economically disadvantaged children.

[5] Results based on Education's *Early Childhood Longitudinal Study: Kindergarten Class of 1998-1999* data from 1998-2007.

[6] The ECLS-K dataset did not allow us to identify homelessness as a student characteristic. The poverty threshold for a family of four in 2009 was $21,954.

[7] Under NSLP, the Department of Agriculture reimburses schools for providing nutritious free or reduced-price lunches to low-income students. The Supplemental Nutrition Assistance Program is the new name for the federal food stamp program. TANF is a federally funded block grant—administered by the Department of Health and Human Services—that is designed to help needy families achieve self-sufficiency.

[8] This difference is statistically significant at the 90 percent confidence level. There were no statistically significant differences for the other racial groups.

[9] According to a GAO report issued in June 2010, "Programs' definitions of homelessness range from including primarily people in homeless shelters or on the street to also including those living with others because of economic hardship." See GAO, *Homelessness: A Common Vocabulary Could Help Agencies Collaborate and Collect More Consistent Data*, GAO-10-702 (Washington, D.C.: June 30, 2010).

[10] These results are from the *National Assessment of Educational Progress (NAEP)*, which collects data on 4th, 8th, and 12th graders. In this section, we present data on eighth graders to be consistent with the eighth grade results we report using the ECLS-K data. In appendix III, we also present information on fourth and eighth graders from the NAEP.

[11] Many of the studies that met the criteria for inclusion in our review controlled for a variety of factors that can affect a student's academic achievement, such as socioeconomic status, parental education, urban or rural school location, and parental marital status. All of the studies we reviewed on academic achievement controlled for students' level of achievement prior to changing schools to account for any pre-existing differences between more mobile and less mobile students. While homelessness may be one of many reasons why students change schools, none of the studies we reviewed included homelessness as a potential factor that could affect student achievement.

[12] Each study we reviewed used its own method to define what constituted "more" or "less" mobile.

[13] A meta-analysis is a statistical analysis of a collection of studies for the purpose of integrating the results.

[14] Many studies focused exclusively on low income, minority students in an urban area and did not compare students of different income levels.

[15] The long-term gain in academic achievement when changing to schools across districts was true for all demographic groups except African Americans. The study authors propose that long-term gains in achievement are due to switching into schools of higher quality, and they suggest that African Americans who switch into nonurban schools do not generally experience as large an increase in school quality as do white and Hispanic students who

switch into non-urban schools. The authors did not explore the factors underlying why African Americans did not experience similar gains.

[16] Under the Individuals with Disabilities Education Act, once a child is determined to be eligible for special education services, an Individualized Education Program is prepared for that child which includes, among other things, an assessment of the child's current educational performance, a statement of measurable performance goals, and a description of the special services that will be provided to the child. 20 U.S.C. § 1414(d).

[17] 20 U.S.C. § 6301.

[18] Pub. L. No. 111-5 (2009).

[19] 20 U.S.C. § 1400 et seq.

[20] 42 U.S.C. § 1751 et seq. (school lunch programs) and 42 U.S.C. § 1771 (child nutrition programs).

[21] 42 U.S.C. § 11431 et seq.

[22] 42 U.S.C. § 11432(e)(3)(E)(i)(III).

[23] 20 U.S.C. § 6391-6399. None of the schools we visited received funding from the Migrant Education Program.

[24] According to Education officials, the Records Exchange Advice, Communication, and Technical Support provides technical assistance on record exchange to state and local officials. Also, Education awards Consortium Incentive Grants to states for activities to improve intrastate and interstate coordination of migrant education programs.

[25] NAEP also collects information on school environment and students' academic achievement. The grades surveyed by NAEP were chosen because they represent critical junctures in academic achievement.

[26] This question asked the respondent to exclude students who transferred into the school during the school year.

[27] Title I, Part A of ESEA is the federal government's largest program for disadvantaged students, including students from low-income families.

[28] The National School Lunch Program is a federal program that provides free and reduced- price lunch to students from low-income families.

[29] We searched the following electronic databases: Education Resources Information Center, ProQuest, ECO/EconLit/SocAbs, PsycINFO, Social SciSearch, Wilson Social Sciences Abstracts, MEDLINE, and Academic OneFile.

[30] A meta-analysis is a statistical analysis of a collection of studies for the purpose of integrating the results.

[31] Six studies assessed both academic and nonacademic outcomes.

INDEX

A

abuse, ix, 1, 3, 4, 6, 7, 19, 23, 25, 27, 29, 34, 36, 37, 38, 39, 40, 41, 42, 43, 44, 45, 46, 47, 48, 49, 50, 51, 52, 53, 54, 55, 57, 58, 59, 60, 61, 62
academic performance, 83, 97, 121
access, 8, 23, 32, 33, 36, 41, 55, 63, 72, 86, 89
accreditation, 32
administrators, 8, 16, 25, 32, 42, 43, 47, 48, 50, 55, 58, 63
African Americans, 125
African-American, 75, 83, 103, 115, 117, 119, 120, 122
age, 27, 77, 82, 91, 117, 120
agencies, 5, 34, 85
Alaska, 66
American Recovery and Reinvestment Act, 70, 87
American Recovery and Reinvestment Act of 2009, 70, 87
arrest, 3, 11, 14, 15, 17, 20, 21, 22, 29, 31, 33
arrests, 20, 33
assault, 23, 25, 27, 51
assessment, 94, 105, 125
athletes, 18
Attorney General, 3, 14, 20, 21
audit, 72, 100
authorities, 8, 19, 23, 25, 27, 65

authority, 19, 36

B

benefits, 74
bias, 115

C

case studies, x, 2, 5, 7, 9
case study, 66
Census, 101
certificate, 3, 16, 17, 28, 30, 36, 37, 38, 39, 43, 45, 62, 66
certification, 25, 29, 30, 36
challenges, ix, x, 67, 68, 71, 84, 93, 99
Chicago, 117, 119, 120, 122
child abuse, 6, 23, 33, 36, 39, 40, 41, 42, 43, 44, 48, 49, 50, 51, 52, 53, 54, 55, 57, 58, 59, 61
child molesters, 5
child pornography, 16, 25, 27, 51
child protection, 34
child protective services, 7, 37, 46
children, ix, 1, 3, 4, 6, 7, 8, 9, 11, 15, 27, 31, 32, 33, 36, 37, 38, 40, 41, 42, 43, 44, 46, 47, 53, 55, 57, 58, 59, 62, 63, 65, 66, 70, 77, 81, 82, 85, 86, 87, 88, 89, 90, 91, 117, 119, 120, 122, 124
classes, 84, 86

classroom, 16, 24, 27, 84, 85
clothing, 69, 87
cognitive development, 91
communities, 4
community, 85, 99, 116, 117
computer, 7, 15, 23
conference, 97
confidentiality, 23
conflict, 82
confrontation, 25
consulting, 20
conversations, 3, 8, 16, 17, 26, 29, 30
convicted sex offenders, ix, x, 2, 4
conviction, x, 2, 3, 5, 11, 14, 18, 20, 21, 22, 27, 33, 36, 38, 39, 40, 41, 48, 50, 63, 66
coordination, 125
cost, 8, 9, 13
counsel, 23
counseling, 18
court documents, x, 2, 3, 5, 18
covering, 5, 98
crimes, 9, 14, 34, 36, 49, 58, 63
criminal conviction, x, 2, 5, 66

D

danger, 65
data analysis, 71
data collection, 94, 98
database, 30, 31, 93
demographic characteristics, 99
dental clinics, 88
Department of Agriculture, 87, 90, 124
Department of Education, ix, x, 1, 4, 14, 20, 21, 28, 34, 37, 39, 41, 43, 53, 58, 61, 68, 71, 89, 93
Department of Health and Human Services, 91, 124
Department of Justice, 5, 21, 31, 34, 65
disadvantaged students, 69, 71, 84, 86, 87, 99, 125
disclosure, 27, 65
distribution, 34, 89
District of Columbia, x, 2, 5, 31, 32, 33, 65
DOJ, 5

domestic violence, 86, 88
donations, 90
draft, 93

E

economic downturn, ix, x, 67, 70, 71, 99
economic status, ix, 68, 115
education, ix, 18, 34, 42, 44, 65, 68, 69, 70, 71, 72, 79, 82, 84, 85, 86, 87, 88, 89, 90, 96, 97, 99, 100, 112, 124, 125
educational opportunities, 124
educational qualifications, 27
educators, 34, 37, 44, 47, 55, 60, 61
Elementary and Secondary Education Act of 1965 (ESEA), x, 67, 70
elementary school, 72, 85, 94, 119
emotional well-being, 68, 82, 83
employees, x, 2, 3, 5, 7, 8, 10, 11, 12, 15, 21, 22, 28, 31, 32, 33, 34, 36, 37, 38, 39, 40, 41, 42, 43, 44, 45, 46, 47, 48, 49, 50, 51, 52, 53, 54, 55, 56, 57, 58, 59, 60, 61, 62, 63, 66
employers, 3, 5, 7, 8, 24, 65
employment, ix, x, 2, 3, 4, 5, 6, 11, 12, 13, 14, 15, 16, 20, 21, 22, 23, 27, 28, 29, 31, 33, 36, 37, 38, 40, 41, 42, 50, 51, 52, 54, 56, 59, 60, 61, 62, 63, 65, 70, 85
employment of sex offenders, x, 2, 4, 5, 6, 31
employment status, 13
endangered, 46, 65
enforcement, x, 2, 5, 7, 11, 22, 26, 27, 30, 34, 36, 38, 39, 40, 42, 44, 45, 46, 47, 48, 49, 50, 51, 53, 54, 55, 57, 58, 59, 60, 61, 62, 63, 65
enrollment, 93
environment, 85, 88, 95, 125
equal opportunity, 86, 89
ethnic groups, 76
evidence, 7, 11, 12, 19, 26, 27, 30, 72, 82, 100
exclusion, 47
exploitation, 29, 36
exposure, 17, 29

Index

F

faith, 40
families, 65, 68, 69, 70, 72, 74, 76, 81, 82, 85, 86, 88, 91, 101, 102, 105, 124, 125
family income, 74, 95
FBI, 36, 40, 41, 42, 43, 44, 45, 46, 48, 49, 50, 51, 52, 53, 54, 55, 56, 58, 61, 62, 63
federal authorities, 25, 27
Federal Bureau of Investigation, 31
federal funds, 124
federal government, 77, 125
federal law, xi, 4, 31, 68, 72
federal programs, x, 67, 69, 71, 86, 93, 99, 100
financial, 81
fingerprints, 16, 20, 21, 22, 28, 65
fiscal year 2009, 89, 90, 91
fishing, 89
food, 28, 86, 87, 90, 95, 102, 103, 124
foreign exchange, 16, 26
funding, 65, 77, 86, 87, 88, 108, 125
funds, 32, 69, 86, 87, 89, 124

G

GAO, ix, x, 1, 2, 3, 4, 14, 20, 34, 64, 65, 67, 68, 69, 70, 74, 75, 76, 78, 79, 80, 91, 107, 108, 109, 110, 111, 112, 113, 114, 123, 124
generalizability, 98
geography, 105
Georgia, 66
gifted, 85
grades, 84, 105, 125
grand jury, 25
grants, 90
graph, 75
guidance, 85, 99
guidance counselors, 85
guilty, 13, 16, 19, 25, 27, 29

H

harassment, 26
Hawaii, 66
health, 46, 60, 85, 88, 91
Health and Human Services, 50, 91, 124
health care, 85
health services, 88
high school, 14, 17, 24, 29, 30, 68, 71, 72, 73, 81, 82, 85, 99
hiring, 3, 10, 11, 16, 20, 24, 38, 65
history, x, 2, 3, 4, 6, 8, 9, 10, 11, 12, 13, 14, 15, 16, 17, 18, 21, 22, 27, 28, 29, 30, 31, 32, 33, 36, 37, 38, 39, 40, 41, 42, 45, 46, 47, 48, 49, 50, 51, 52, 53, 54, 55, 56, 57, 58, 59, 60, 61, 62, 63, 66, 105
homelessness, ix, x, 67, 70, 124
homeowners, 81
homes, 81, 82
House of Representatives, 1, 4
household income, 101
housing, 70, 85
human, 22, 26, 39, 65
human resources, 65
Hurricane Katrina, 17, 29

I

identification, 84, 94
identity, 5
immunization, 84
income, 68, 69, 72, 73, 77, 81, 84, 86, 87, 89, 90, 91, 95, 96, 98, 100, 101, 116, 120, 121, 124, 125
individuals, ix, x, 2, 5, 6, 11, 22, 32, 44, 45, 46, 49, 60
Individuals with Disabilities Education Act, 69, 87, 90, 125
industry, 81
information sharing, 21
injury, 21, 36, 47
intercourse, 25
intervention, 87, 90, 120
Iowa, 66

104 Index

issues, 24, 82, 86, 99, 100

J

Japan, 25
junior high school, 85

K

kidnapping, 51
kindergarten, ix, 1, 5, 68, 76, 84, 94

L

language proficiency, 84
law enforcement, x, 2, 5, 7, 11, 22, 26, 27, 30, 34, 36, 37, 38, 39, 40, 42, 43, 44, 45, 46, 47, 48, 49, 50, 51, 53, 54, 55, 57, 58, 59, 60, 61, 62, 63, 65
laws, ix, x, xi, 2, 4, 5, 6, 10, 16, 26, 31, 32, 64, 68, 72, 100
lawyers, 26
learning, 88
lesson plan, 88
living arrangements, 77
Louisiana, 3, 8, 10, 17, 29, 30, 66

M

majority, 31, 33, 73
maltreatment, 36
man, 20, 29
marital status, 124
Maryland, 16, 25, 26, 66
measurement, 97
mental health, 46, 60
meta-analysis, 71, 83, 97, 125, 126
methodology, 72, 93
Mexico, 29, 66
minority students, 73, 120, 125
minors, 9, 15, 37, 41, 44, 46, 49, 54, 55, 59, 60, 62, 63
Missouri, 66

modules, 88
Montana, 66
murder, 51

N

NAEP, 69, 78, 79, 80, 94, 95, 96, 105, 107, 108, 109, 110, 111, 112, 113, 114, 124, 125
National Assessment of Educational Progress, 69, 94, 95, 105, 124
National Center for Education Statistics, 69, 93
National Center for Education Statistics (NCES), 93
National Center for Missing and Exploited Children, 4
National Crime Information Center, 31
National Research Council, 123
National School Lunch Program, 69, 74, 96, 125
National Sex Offender Registry, x, 2, 5
negative effects, 83
neglect, 36, 38, 39, 40, 42, 43, 45, 46, 48, 49, 50, 51, 53, 54, 55, 57, 59, 60, 61, 62
networking, 26
No Child Left Behind, 70, 73
nutrition, 87, 125

O

offenders, ix, x, 2, 3, 4, 6, 9, 10, 11, 14, 22, 31, 32, 36, 37, 38, 40, 41, 42, 43, 44, 45, 47, 48, 49, 50, 51, 52, 54, 55, 56, 57, 59, 60, 61, 62, 63, 65
Office of Justice Programs, 65
officials, x, 2, 3, 5, 7, 8, 9, 10, 11, 13, 14, 15, 18, 19, 20, 21, 22, 24, 26, 27, 28, 30, 33, 36, 38, 39, 40, 47, 49, 51, 53, 59, 68, 69, 71, 76, 81, 84, 85, 86, 87, 88, 94, 99, 100, 105, 125
Oklahoma, 66
opportunities, 124
outreach, 86, 88

Index

P

Pacific, 121
pairing, 96
parenting, 86
parents, 18, 26, 34, 38, 54, 59, 71, 73, 81, 85, 88, 94, 99, 100, 102, 103, 104, 105, 119, 121
parole, 46, 50, 51, 54, 60
permission, , 45, 46, 49
personal problems, 24
personality, 19
photographs, 25, 26, 27, 65
physical abuse, ix, 1, 43
physical abuse of children, ix, 1
police, 3, 5, 13, 14, 16, 18, 19, 20, 21, 22, 25, 26, 27, 29
policy, 6, 10, 17, 32, 54, 57
policymakers, 73
population, 4, 68, 69, 71, 73, 77, 81, 88, 94, 95, 115, 116, 117, 119, 120, 121, 122
poverty, 71, 74, 95, 99, 101, 124
preparation, iv, 70, 100
preschool, 55
prevention, 6, 65
private schools, ix, 1, 2, 4, 6, 9, 29, 31, 33, 36, 41, 44, 46, 47, 48, 57, 58, 61
probability, 94
probability sampling, 94
professionals, 48, 65
protection, 34
public concern, 4
public concerns, 4
public education, 89
public safety, 9, 13
public schools, 3, 11, 12, 15, 17, 22, 32, 33, 61
punishment, 7

Q

qualifications, 27

R

race, 83, 95, 104
rape, 61
reading, 68, 72, 73, 82, 105
real estate, 81
reasoning, 84
reasoning skills, 84
recognition, 43
recommendations, iv, 7, 8, 23, 24, 28, 68
redundancy, 98
Registry, x, 2, 5, 38
regulations, 6, 18, 72, 100
relatives, 76, 82
reliability, 94, 98
rent, 76, 81, 105
requirements, x, 2, 6, 13, 15, 16, 18, 21, 22, 28, 31, 32, 33, 36, 37, 38, 40, 42, 51, 52, 54, 56, 59, 60, 63, 65
Residential, 65, 121, 123
resources, 66, 99
response, 11, 15
restrictions, 32, 50
rights, 23
risk, 4, 13, 65, 69, 77, 121
routines, 85

S

safety, 9, 13, 82
scholarship, 32
school districts, xi, 18, 23, 24, 32, 54, 57, 68, 71, 83, 85, 87, 88, 99
school employee, ix, x, 1, 2, 3, 5, 7, 15, 20, 22, 28, 32, 33, 34, 36, 37, 38, 39, 40, 42, 43, 44, 46, 47, 48, 49, 51, 52, 53, 54, 55, 56, 58, 59, 60, 61, 62, 63, 66
school enrollment, 93
science, 73, 98, 105
scope, 70, 72, 93, 98, 115, 116, 117, 118, 119, 121
secondary schools, 124
security, 5
self-sufficiency, 124

Senate, 70

services, 7, 8, 15, 39, 40, 43, 46, 55, 61, 65, 72, 77, 79, 82, 84, 85, 87, 88, 90, 91, 109, 125

SES, 115, 117, 119, 120, 122

sex, ix, x, 2, 3, 4, 5, 6, 8, 10, 11, 12, 13, 14, 15, 17, 18, 20, 21, 22, 25, 27, 29, 30, 31, 36, 37, 38, 40, 42, 43, 44, 45, 47, 48, 49, 51, 52, 54, 55, 56, 57, 58, 59, 60, 61, 63, 65

sex offenders, ix, x, 2, 4, 5, 6, 8, 10, 11, 22, 31, 36, 37, 38, 40, 42, 43, 44, 45, 47, 48, 49, 51, 52, 54, 55, 56, 57, 59, 60, 61, 63, 65

sexual abuse, ix, 1, 4, 25, 27, 29, 34, 36, 45, 47, 58, 61, 62

sexual assaults, 4, 49

sexual contact, 3, 10, 16, 27

sexual intercourse, 25

sexual misconduct, ix, x, 1, 2, 3, 4, 5, 6, 7, 62

social capital, 98

social security, 5

social services, 82

social support network, 85

social workers, 99

socioeconomic status, 82, 124

South Dakota, 66

special education, 68, 69, 79, 84, 87, 90, 96, 112, 125

staff development, 87

standard error, 94

state, ix, x, 2, 4, 5, 6, 9, 10, 12, 13, 16, 18, 19, 21, 23, 25, 27, 28, 30, 31, 32, 33, 34, 36, 37, 38, 39, 40, 41, 42, 43, 44, 45, 46, 47, 48, 49, 50, 51, 52, 54, 55, 57, 58, 59, 60, 61, 62, 63, 64, 71, 73, 84, 86, 88, 89, 97, 99, 125

state authorities, 23

state laws, ix, x, 2, 5, 6, 10, 64

states, x, 2, 4, 5, 10, 12, 31, 32, 33, 65, 71, 81, 84, 86, 88, 90, 99, 125

statistics, 5, 94

statutes, 18, 33

statutory provisions, 6

student achievement, 125

student teacher, 40, 45, 60

summer program, 87

supervision, 54, 62

supervisors, 14

Supplemental Nutrition Assistance Program, 74, 124

support staff, 2, 6, 9

synthesis, 97

T

teachers, 2, 3, 6, 7, 8, 17, 23, 29, 30, 32, 33, 36, 37, 38, 39, 40, 41, 42, 43, 44, 45, 47, 48, 49, 50, 51, 53, 54, 55, 57, 58, 59, 60, 61, 62, 63, 65, 69, 76, 81, 82, 84, 85, 86, 94, 99

teams, 10, 17

technical assistance, 125

techniques, 94

technology, 87

tenure, 11, 20, 21

test scores, 84, 98

testing, 14

threatening behavior, 26

Title I, 72, 77, 78, 86, 89, 96, 108, 109, 124, 125

training, 87, 98

transportation, 69, 86, 87

treatment, ix, 1, 4

trial, 17

tutoring, 69, 86, 87, 88

U

U.S. history, 105

United, vii, 1, 4, 25, 67, 70, 97

United States, vii, 1, 4, 25, 67, 70, 97

urban, 71, 82, 83, 99, 115, 116, 117, 119, 120, 122, 124, 125

urban areas, 83

urban schools, 125

V

variables, 105
victims, 4, 41, 44, 46, 47, 49, 50, 54, 55, 59,
 60, 62, 63
videos, 3, 26, 27
violence, 82, 86, 88
violent offenders, 61

W

walking, 29
Washington, 65, 66, 123, 124
welfare, 38, 42, 46, 48, 51, 60, 63
well-being, 68, 82, 83
Wisconsin, 13, 66
withdrawal, 84
workers, 8, 11, 88, 99